Published by Periplus Editions (HK) Ltd.
with editorial offices at
153 Milk Street
Boston MA 02109, and
5 Little Road #08-01
Singapore 536983

ISBN: 962-593-998-9

Library of Congress
Card Number: 00-107033

Publisher: Eric Oey
Associate Publisher: Christina Ong
Editor: Philip Tatham
Recipe testing: Devagi Sanmugam
Production: Violet Wong

Distributed by

North America and Europe
Tuttle Publishing
Distribution Center
Airport Industrial Park
364 Innovation Drive
North Clarendon, VT 05759-9436
Tel: (802) 773-8930
Fax: (802) 773-6993

Japan
Tuttle Publishing
RK Building 2nd Floor
2-13-10 Shimo Meguro, Meguro-Ku
Tokyo 153 0064, Japan
Tel: (81-3) 5437-0171
Fax: (81-3) 5437-0755

Asia Pacific
Berkeley Books Pte. Ltd.
5 Little Road #08-01
Singapore 536983
Tel: (65) 280-1330
Fax: (65) 280-6290

Photo credits
All food and location photography by Luca Invernizzi
Tettoni. Additional photos by Jill Gocher, p. 9; and
Dominic Sansoni, pp. 3 (above), 4, 8, 10–15, 20, 25.

First edition
1 3 5 7 9 10 8 6 4 2
06 05 04 03 02 01
PRINTED IN SINGAPORE

THE FOOD OF
SRI LANKA

Authentic Recipes from the Isle of Gems

by Douglas Bullis and Wendy Hutton
Photography by Luca Invernizzi Tettoni

PERIPLUS

Contents

Part One: Food in Sri Lanka

Cinnamon, cloves, and other spices are the island's culinary gemstones

Douglas Bullis

Sri Lanka, the fabled island of sapphires, rubies, and other precious stones, is home to one of the least known Asian cuisines. Rarely found in restaurants outside the island itself, Sri Lankan fare is often mistaken for yet another Indian regional cuisine. To the culinary explorer, however, Sri Lankan food is as intriguing and unique as the many other customs of this island paradise.

Sri Lanka, formerly known as Ceylon, is located off India's southeast coast. The rugged terrain of the central highlands—characterized by high mountains and plateaus, steep river gorges, and swathes of tea plantations—dominates much of the island. This falls away to sandy lowlands, rice paddies, and long stretches of palm-fringed beaches.

The ancestors of today's Sinhalese peoples arrived some 2,500 years ago from Northern India. They named themselves after a mythic ancestor who was born of a *sinha* (lion) and a princess. After conquering the local Yakshas, a succession of kingdoms—Sinhalese in the center and south, and Tamil in the Jaffna Peninsula—rose and fell over the centuries. The first Portuguese ships chanced upon Sri Lanka in the early sixteenth century and set about trading in cinnamon and other spices. There followed four hundred years of Western presence in the form of Portuguese, Dutch, and finally the British before Sri Lanka regained her independence in 1948.

Such diverse influences may be tasted in dishes of Arab *biryani* (yellow rice with meat and nuts), Malay *nasi kuning* (turmeric rice), Portuguese love cakes, and Dutch *breuders* (dough cakes) and *lampries* (savory rice and meat packets).

Sri Lankan cuisine, which is based upon rice with vegetable, fish, or meat curries, and a variety of side dishes and condiments, reflects the geographical and ethnic differences of the land. Seafood dishes, such as *seer* fish stew, *ambulthiyal* (sour claypot fish), crab curry, and Jaffna *kool* (Tamil seafood soup), are common to coastal and, increasingly, inland areas. The eating of large animals, such as cows and deer, is less popular due to the predominantly Buddhist and Hindu population; chicken and freshwater fish are usually preferred instead.

Sri Lanka is also blessed with an abundant harvest of fruits and vegetables. Jackfruit, breadfruit, okra, gourds, plantains, and drumsticks are but some of the vegetables, tubers, and leaves that feature in one or other Sri Lankan dish.

It is a cuisine expressed in spices—cinnamon, cloves, nutmeg, coriander, mace, pepper, cardamom, red chiles, mustard seeds, cumin, fenugreek, and turmeric are all used to flavor curries, while some add flavor to desserts and cakes. The spices of Sri Lanka, which helped to shape the history of the island, are truly its culinary gemstones.

Page 2:
The beginning of a wedding procession in the south of Sri Lanka is reenacted by cultural dancers.
Opposite:
A festive display of Sri Lankan rice, sambols, and fish curries.

Gustatory Geography

The fruits of land and sea are in equal abundance on this paradise isle

Douglas Bullis

Sri Lanka's dry and wet seasons are reversed from one side of the island to the other by two monsoons. From May to August, the southwest monsoon, Yala, brings heavy rain to the southern, western, and central highland regions, leaving the other side dry. From October to January, the gentler northeast monsoon, Maha, brings rain to the north of the island. The coastal regions are hot and humid year round, while the hill country feels like perpetual spring.

When Sri Lanka's first settlers arrived from India in about 500 BC, the coastal lowlands they found were no paradise. Undaunted, they set to work making them one. They had brought with them the techniques of turning a stream into a small pond, and of digging sluices with gates to let water into small fields on demand. What happened over the next ten centuries is one of the greatest irrigation feats in world history: Sri Lanka's system of reservoir "tanks" feeding a latticework of watercourses produced a rice surplus so large that it financed the island's architectural and sculptural splendors.

The simple brown rice of those early times became the twenty-odd varieties grown today. The two monsoons translate to two harvests a year over much of the island. Low-country rice is mostly plain white rice that cooks easily and has no strong taste to distract from the curries. Somewhat upscale is a red rice that bursts as it cooks, yielding a fluffy white interior with reddish flecks on the surface—this is the festive *suduru samba* served when entertaining guests. The highest grade of rice is long-grained basmati, often used when aromatic dishes are desired. In between, many lesser varieties are grown, usually in small quantities for local use.

However, paddy agriculture is far from the only kind of farming. Slash-and-burn, or *chena* farming, is the bane of the back country, as it produces only two or three harvests of millet and root vegetables before depleting the soils and forcing the farmer to move on. But for many poor people, it is the only choice.

In a category all of its own is the island's enormous production of tea. The nuances of Sri Lankan tea are as complex and sophisticated as the nuances of fine wine. Small family plantations can be found even a few miles inland from the coast, but the higher the plantation the better the tea. The premium Dambula and other highland teas grow on tidily pruned plantations that undulate over the landscape as gracefully as slow-flowing water. The teas are processed in multi-story factories painted white or silver that stand out amid the landscape like ghosts on a green sea.

Up to fifty fishers start at dawn and take four to six hours to bring in a purse net with its rich harvest of reef fish.

A tapper collects sap from a kitul palm tree to be made into jaggery, the kitul palm sugar that sweetens so many Sri Lankan dishes.

too seriously. Visitors to these professional spiceries are treated to a fabulous bouquet of odors as they learn all about how spices are grown and prepared for consumers the world over.

A final glance at the country's agriculture focuses on the men who walk ropeways high in the sky doing the dangerous job of harvesting drippings from the flowers of the kitul palm. Treading gingerly along a single rope and guyline fifty feet or more above the ground, they tie shut the tips of the kitul's flowers with cord so they cannot open. The sap, which ordinarily would go into swelling the flower and then filling its fruit, instead oozes into clay pots tied to the flower's stem. Every few days these are visited by the tappers, who empty the juice into a pot slung around their waists.

The resulting treacle has a unique flavor which matches superbly with Sri Lanka's high-butterfat but bland curd or buffalo-milk yoghurt. When the treacle is hardened by boiling and then cooled, it becomes jaggery, the most popular sweetener on the island and an essential ingredient in most Sri Lankan desserts and sweetmeats.

A close cousin of this process does the same with coconut flowers. The frothy white sap ferments into toddy or *ra*, a foamy white alcohol that can be drunk as is, or distilled into arrack. *Ra* is such a staple that it even lent its name to a town on the Colombo–Kandy railway line, Ragama—literally "Toddy Town."

The sea's bounty includes several kinds of tuna, plus grouper, whitefish, kingfish, barracuda, trevally, squid, octopus, and a host of lesser species. One of the most popular fish in Sri Lanka is the *seer* or

And of course one can't overlook the island's spice gardens. The gaily proclaimed ones along the highways to Kandy are for tourists. The serious spice plantations growing for export are found in moist valleys or hilly areas. Be they for tourist or export, the goods are the same: over here spindly, weedy bushes whose flower yields a darkish nubbin that dries into clove; over there bushy nutmeg trees with bright tan fruit.

The delicate seed pods of the cardamom grow symbiotically under clove plants. Gangly peppercorns cluster under the long leaves of their plant, looking rather like grape bunches that took their diet

Spanish mackerel which is cooked in many styles.

Most fishing is done from old-fashioned *oruwa* dugout outrigger canoes lashed together with coconut-fiber twine. The old handmade *katta maran* (literally "big logs," and the origin of the word "catamaran") dugouts come in various hues of salt-toughened wood. Their crews divide between "netters" and "chummers," the latter a term for hook-and-line fishers that was borrowed from the British.

The fish left over after those for household use are sold to itinerant hawkers who have mounted wide wooden boxes on the back of bicycles. They wobble their way into the countryside, fish tails sticking out either side of the box, calling out "Lu! Lu!" (short for *malu*, the Sinhalese word for fish).

A drive along the coastal highway passes one ramshackle wooden roadside stall after the other with gorgeous rows of tuna lined up like cordwood. They also sell squid, *seer*, kingfish, slabs of shark big enough to cover a dinner plate, and tiny silver sprats that are dried and munched like popcorn.

Other stalls display freshly caught skipjacks drying in the sun. Although the chewy locally-dried tuna is often referred to as "Maldive fish," the authentic Maldive fish used in restaurants is tougher than dried leather.

The most idiosyncratic of Sri Lanka's fishermen are the island's famous stilt fishers. These men wedge sturdy poles into rock crevices in the shallows, to which they attach a tiny sling-net that passes for a seat. While the catch is modest, some of the brilliantly colored coral-dwellers they bring in, such as the striped mullet, are among the tastiest on the island.

Another fishing style is net casting. Fishermen patrol tidal pools and rocky ledges in the late afternoon in search of the parrotfish or trevallly hungry enough to let down its guard as night approaches. Netters have hurling styles so unique that locals can identify someone at a distance by the way he throws his net.

Mangoes, coconuts, pumpkin, and bananas are just some of the fruits and vegetables available from roadside stalls such as this.

One Land, Many Peoples

Sri Lanka's multiethnic population ensures culinary variety

Wendy Hutton

Sri Lanka boasts a vast array of tropical fruits, vegetables, and spices, as well as an abundance of fish and other seafood in its lakes, rivers, and seas, and wild game in its forests. The way Sri Lankans put this bounty together in the kitchen depends to some extent on where they live, and even more upon their ethnic and religious background.

The multiethnic mix of people living on this small island comprises Sinhalese, Tamils, Moors (Muslims), Burghers and Eurasians, Malays, and Veddhas.

The majority of the population are Sinhalese, believed to be descended from Indo-Aryans who arrived from northern India more than 2,000 years ago and intermarried with scattered groups of tribal Veddhas. Over the centuries, the cooking of the Sinhalese has evolved into two slightly different styles: coastal or "low country" Sinhalese, and Kandy or "upcountry" Sinhalese.

Regardless of where they live, the staple food for Sinhalese (and indeed, for all Sri Lankans) is rice. This is usually accompanied by a range of spiced vegetables, fish, poultry, meat, or game dishes. Most Sinhalese are Buddhist, and although the taking of life is against Buddhist teachings, most Sinhalese don't mind eating food which has been killed by others. Strict Buddhists, however, are vegetarian (something they share with a number of Hindu Tamils).

In coastal Sinhalese cuisine, fish, and other seafood feature far more widely than poultry or meat, and coconut milk is the preferred base for curries. Towns such as Bentota, Chilaw, and Batticaloa are noted for excellent seafood but most famous of all is Negombo. The crab and shrimp dishes from this west coast town are well-known throughout Sri Lanka. Negombo is also the site of one of the island's busiest and most colorful fish markets.

Another Sinhalese specialty from the coast is *ambulthiyal*, or sour claypot fish. At its best in the Southern town of Ambalangoda, *ambulthiyal* is a dish of *balaya* (bonito) which uses *goraka* (gamboge) as both a flavoring and a preservative—even in Sri Lanka's heat and humidity, this dish can keep for up to a week.

An ingredient known as Maldive fish is widely used as a seasoning throughout Sri Lanka, but especially in coastal regions. It is made from a type of bonito (also known as skipjack) which is boiled, smoked, and sun-dried until it is rock hard.

Kandy, the heart of upcountry Sri Lanka, remained an independent Sinhalese kingdom until the British finally took over in 1815, thus it largely escaped the social and culinary influences of the Portuguese and Dutch. Thanks to the higher altitude

Stilt fishermen wedge wooden poles into rock crevices to use as a perch while fishing.

and cooler climate, a wide range of vegetables and fruits flourish around Kandy and other upcountry regions, which are renowned for their range of delicious vegetable dishes.

Many Kandian curries are made with unusual ingredients such as young jackfruit, jackfruit seeds, cashews, breadfruit, and green papaya, while various edible flowers such as turmeric, hibiscus, and sesbania may end up in an omelette or curry. Game, including deer and wild birds, was also an upcountry favorite, although dwindling forests and

A street vendor prepares kaum (left) and kokis (right), two traditional deep-fried snacks or sweetmeats as they are known in Sri Lanka.

restrictions on hunting in protected areas have diminished the amount of game now being cooked in upcountry kitchens.

Sinhalese refer to their main meal as "rice and curry," and normally serve several types of spiced or "curried" dishes of vegetables, fish, meat, or poultry. Curries are classified by their spicing and method of cooking rather than by their main ingredient. Thus, there are "red" curries which contain an often incendiary amount of chile, and usually a limited number of spices. There are also the distinctively Sinhalese "black" curries which develop a wonderfully rich aroma and flavor, thanks to the technique of roasting whole spices (primarily coriander, cumin, and fennel) to a rich brown color before grinding them. "Brown" curries are made from unroasted spices, while "white" curries, which contain plenty of coconut milk and very little chile, are generally quite mild.

When choosing which curries to serve with the rice, Sinhalese cooks ensure that there is a variety of textures as well as flavors, with at least one fairly liquid, or soupy, curry to help moisten the rice, and usually a relatively dry curry with a thick gravy. One of the curries will most likely be a spiced lentil dish, and there is sure to be at least one pungent side dish or condiment known as a *sambol* (from the Malay *sambal*). These *sambol*, also know as "rice pullers," are guaranteed to whet the appetite with their basic ingredient—anything from onion to bitter gourd, dried shrimp to salted lime—heightened by the flavors of chile, onion, salt, and Maldive fish.

One of the most popular *sambol*, *pol sambol*, is made with freshly grated coconut; a simple meal of rice, lentils, *pol sambol*, and *mallung* is inexpensive, nutritious, and utterly satisfying. *Mallung*, which provides an unmistakable Sinhalese accent to every meal, is a vitamin- and mineral-packed mixture of leafy greens, freshly grated coconut, lime juice, chile, and powdered Maldive fish. Many of the greens used in a *mallung* are plucked from the kitchen garden, including young passionfruit leaves, *gotu kala* (Asian pennywort), young chile leaves, young leaves from the drumstick tree, and the leaves of the flowering cassia tree.

The first Tamils are believed to have arrived at about the same time as the Indo-Ayrans, around 2,000 years ago. Successive waves of Tamils from southern India established themselves in Sri Lanka, mostly in the north, on the Jaffna peninsula. In the mid to late nineteenth and early twentieth centuries, Tamil laborers were brought in by the British to work on the tea estates in the cooler hilly areas of Sri Lanka. These later arrivals are generally referred to as Indian Tamils, to distinguish them from the long-established Jaffna Tamils.

The majority of Sri Lanka's Tamils are Hindu, therefore they do not eat beef. Indeed, most Jaffna Tamils are strict vegetarians. Vegetables are grown in the gardens of countless families in Jaffna, irrigated by deep wells; anyone who has tasted fresh home-grown vegetables cooked Tamil style is indeed fortunate.

The Tamil dishes found in Sri Lanka are similar to those of southeast India, where the vegetarian cuisine is among the world's finest. As with Sinhalese food, the basis of Tamil food is influenced by the teachings of the Ayurveda, ancient texts on the "wisdom of life and longevity." Seasonings such as curry leaves, brown mustard seed, and dried chiles are widely used, while freshly grated coconut, coconut milk, and yoghurt appear in many vegetable dishes.

Popular Tamil dishes found in Sri Lanka include *rasam*, a spicy sour soup that is an aid to digestion; *kool*, a thick seafood soup originating from Jaffna fisherfolk; *vadai*, or deep-fried savories made with black gram flour; and many types of vegetable *pachadi*, where cooked vegetables are tossed with curd or yoghurt, and freshly grated coconut.

A market trader removes the skin from a jackfruit.

Thosai, slightly sour pancakes made with black gram and rice flours, constitute another delicious Tamil contribution to the culinary scene. Some Tamil dishes, such as the steamed rice-flour rolls known as *pittu*, have been adopted by Sinhalese, and are now regarded as Sri Lankan.

Sri Lanka's Muslims are believed to be descended from Arab traders who settled in and around Galle, Beruwala, and Puttalam from as early as the eighth century, and from Indian Muslims who migrated from southwest India.

Ingredients such as rose water, saffron (not to be confused with turmeric, which is often called "saffron" or "Indian saffron" in Sri Lanka), cashews, and mint, as well as dishes like biryani rice, korma curries, and *faluda* (a dessert of cornflour and water) all reflect Arab or Indian Muslim influence on Sri Lanka's cuisine. Arabs are also credited with planting the first coffee trees—native to the Arabian peninsula—in Sri Lanka.

In general, Muslim food is slightly sweeter than Sinhalese and Tamil food, but it certainly isn't lacking in spice. In fact, Arab traders are said to have been responsible for bringing spices such as cloves and nutmeg from the Moluccan islands to Sri Lanka long before the Dutch colonized what they called the Dutch East Indies (now Indonesia). Muslim dishes in Sri Lanka never contain pork, which is forbidden by Islam, and pork is only occasionally eaten by the Christian Tamils and Sinhalese.

In more recent times, Malays, who were brought by the Dutch, have intermarried with the Muslim community and brought with them several dishes which have since become part of the Sri Lankan kitchen. *Sathe* is the Sri Lankan equivalent of satay, or cubes of meat threaded on skewers and served with a peanut and chile sauce. Other Malay dishes include *gula melaka* (sago pudding with jaggery), *nasi kuning* (turmeric rice), *barbuth* (honeycomb tripe curry), *seenakku* and *parsong* (two types of rice flour cakes).

The multiethnic mix of people living on this small island has resulted in a varied and fascinating cuisine that is delicious regardless of the geographic, ethnic, or religious origin.

Colonial Tastes

Portuguese, Dutch, and British influences and the creation of a Burgher culture

Wendy Hutton

The wave of Western expansionism which began at the end of the fifteenth century, when the Portuguese first rounded the Cape of Good Hope and reached the west coast of India, was to have a significant impact on Sri Lanka. Over the next four centuries, colonialism affected not only the agriculture, social structure, and religions of the country, but also the cuisine.

In fact, it was cuisine that attracted the Portuguese in the first place, or to be more precise, spices. With refrigeration and modern methods of food preservation, it is difficult today to imagine how vital and valuable spices were several centuries ago. They were used to help preserve food and also to mask the flavors of food that might not necessarily be in prime condition. Many spices have medicinal properties and some were believed to ward off the plagues that frequently swept through Europe.

The trade in spices—particularly pepper, nutmeg, cloves, cinnamon, and cardamom—was then controlled by Arab merchants, who obtained the spices in various parts of Asia and then sold them to Venetian merchants at exorbitant prices. The search for the source of these valuable spices prompted the Portuguese to set out on their voyages of exploration. Not only did they intend to cut out the Arab middlemen, they were also filled with mis-sionary zeal, intent on obtaining Christian converts.

By the early 1600s, the Portuguese had gained control of the southwest coast of Sri Lanka (which they called Zeilan), and had converted some of the Sinhalese royalty to Catholicism. The island was an important source of revenue, thanks to its spices (particularly cinnamon), and was also an ideal place for Portuguese vessels to take on supplies in their voyages between their colonies of Goa and Malacca.

The Portuguese introduced a number of plants they had discovered in the Americas, the most important being chile, as well as corn, tomatoes, and guavas. It is hard to imagine Sri Lankan cuisine without chile, but prior to the introduction of this taste-tingling plant, all Asians had to rely on pepper for heat. The Portuguese impact on the cuisine of Sri Lanka has lasted until today, but almost exclusively in the area of rich cakes: *bolo de coco* (a coconut cake), *foguete* (deep-fried pastry tubes with a sweet filling) and *bolo folhadao* (a layered cake) are all a legacy of the Portuguese.

By the end of the seventeenth century, the people of Sri Lanka were desperate to oust the Portuguese; they promised the Dutch the monopoly of the rich spice trade if they could get rid of these foreigners who "never took pains to find out what the local laws and customs were."

British colonials celebrate the end of World War II with a victory dinner in Colombo.

However, it proved to be a matter of exchanging one colonial master for another, as the Dutch pushed the Portuguese out and then extended their control over most of the island, except for Kandy, which remained an independent Sinhalese kingdom.

The Dutch—who controlled most of the islands in the Dutch East Indies, and who had followed the Portuguese as rulers of Malacca—brought in a number of Malays to Sri Lanka (there was even a Malay regiment). They also introduced several fruits indigenous to the Malay peninsula, including rambutan, mangosteen, and durian, as well as Malay names for certain dishes, including spicy condiments (*sambol*) and pickles (*achchar*).

Laborers at a spice plantation peel cinnamon bark on the verandah of the factory in 1900.

Like the Portuguese, the Dutch left a number of cakes to become part of the culinary legacy of Sri Lanka, and particularly of the Burgher community, including *breudher,* a rich cake made with yeast.

Dutch meatballs, or *frikadel*, appear as part of a cross-cultural dish served on special occasions in many Sri Lankan homes. *Lampries* (a corruption of the Dutch *lomprijst*) combines these meatballs with a typically Sinhalese curry made with four types of meat and a tangy *sambol*, all wrapped up in a piece of banana leaf and steamed.

Another Dutch recipe, *smore*, or sliced braised beef, has evolved over the years into a version that would not be recognized in Holland, with the meat simmered in spiced coconut milk accented with tamarind juice.

By the end of the eighteenth century, the British, with their superior naval force, had started to push the Dutch out of the island they called Ceylon. However, it took almost another two decades until they managed to topple the independent kingdom of Kandy, and to exert control over the entire island.

The British had by far the greatest impact of any of the colonial rulers. They abolished most of the discriminatory regulations and monopolies established by the Dutch, and brought about a significant change in the island's economy. By the mid-1800s, coffee—planted in the hill country in the interior—had replaced cinnamon as the island's most valuable crop. However, a blight virtually wiped out the coffee plantations in the late 1870s.

Tea seedlings had been imported from China in 1824 and from Assam in 1839, and the first tea estates were established by 1867—just in time to take over in importance after the failure of the coffee crop. The import of large numbers of southern Indian Tamils to work on the coffee and tea estates was another move to have a significant impact on the shape of the country.

Inevitably, as there had been intermarriage between the Portuguese and Dutch and local woman, so too was there intermarriage with the British. However, one observer remarked, in the late 1870s, that the "English, Scotch or German mechanical engineer, road officer or locomotive foreman generally marries the native burgher female with whom he associates; the civil servant, merchant, planter and army officer only keeps her."

The children of these marriages became known, during the Dutch period, as Burghers or "town dwellers." This term was also used for people of Portuguese descent, and later, for those who had British blood. Christian converts were able to escape the social distinctions of the traditional caste system, and the Burghers became a privileged minority.

Burghers, other wealthy locals, and Europeans enjoy an evening at the Orient Club in the early twentieth century.

Their fluency in Dutch, and, later, in English, ensured they found work in various government departments and even as lawyers.

The British influence on Burgher food seems to be limited to the way meals are served. In many Burgher homes, lunch is the universal "curry and rice." However, the evening meal is often served British style, in what is called a "course" dinner. This usually begins with a soup and might be followed by a spiced meat stew, potatoes or bread and vegetables. Many of these dishes are based on Dutch or British recipes, but with sufficient spices and seasonings added to please the palates of those accustomed to more flavorful Sinhalese food.

Spice and Other Things Nice

How cinnamon changed the course of history for Sri Lanka

Wendy Hutton

Spices, so important to the Sri Lankan kitchen, actually helped shape the history of the island. The Portuguese arrived at the beginning of the sixteenth century, and it was Sri Lanka's famous cinnamon—the delicately fragrant bark of the *Cinnamomum zeylanicum* tree native to the island —which became the prime source of revenue for the Europeans.

Sri Lanka's cinnamon trees, which grew wild on the southern and western coasts of the island, were said to produce the finest cinnamon in the world— and sold for three times the price of cinnamon from other regions. It was said that "it healeth, it openeth and strengtheneth the mawe and digesteth the meat; it is also used against all kinde of pyson that may hurt the hart."

Cinnamon was still the most important source of revenue by the time the Dutch seized control of the island. They introduced penalties to protect it, making it a capital offence to damage a plant, and to sell or to export the quills or their oil. The Dutch did eventually succeed in cultivating cin-namon, but still relied largely on the wild supply. By the nineteenth century, however, the supremacy of cinnamon was challenged by the cheaper cassia bark grown elsewhere in Asia. The flavor is far less refined, and cassia bark lacks the faint sweetness of true cinnamon, but as the price was so competitive, Sri Lankan cinnamon eventually lost its dominance.

Cloves and nutmeg, indigenous to the Moluccas in eastern Indonesia, were planted in Sri Lanka by the Dutch who controlled most of the Dutch East Indies. Cardamom, indigenous to both Sri Lanka and southern India, was another valuable spice which flourished in the wetter regions of the country.

All of Sri Lanka's spices are used to flavor savory dishes such as curries; some also add their fragrance and flavor to desserts and cakes. Spices such as cinnamon therefore command a very important position in Sri Lankan culture, not only as culinary flavorings but also by virtue of their having played such a major role in the country's history.

Opposite:
(Clockwise from top left) cinnamon, cloves, nutmeg, coriander, mace, pepper, cardamom, dried red chiles, mustard seeds, cumin, fenugreek, fennel, and turmeric.

Left:
Cinnamon sticks are in fact dried curls of bark which are removed in thin slivers from the Cinnamomum zeylanicum tree. Cassia, which is often sold as cinnamon, comes from a related species and is darker brown in color with a stronger flavor.

Banking on Tea

Or how the word "Ceylon" was immortalized

Douglas Bullis

A serendipitous twist turned a disastrous blight of coffee rust, which swept through the island's coffee estates in the 1870s, into a tea bonanza: the pretty but unassuming little bush became Sri Lanka's chief export and immortalized the word "Ceylon." A few tea plants brought from China took very well to the cool, crisp highland climate of the Looloocondrie Estate near Kandy. The island's planters were much relieved to find that tea plants love the same climate that coffee does, and that tea has just as enthusiastic a following all around the world.

Converting a green leaf into a tasty brown beverage is a quite a story in inorganic chemistry. Yet it is an everyday event in the slab-sided white or aluminum-painted tea factories that dot the flowing hills. These are slatted with louvers to hasten the drying process. Within them the three steps of withering, grinding, and fermenting convert the fresh leaves to a moist, black mass, which is then heated in a stove to reduce to two percent all the moisture originally contained in the leaf.

Once broken into flakes, tea is graded into names based on the size of the flake. These names have the kind of arcane character often emanating from professionals when talking to each other. In the case of tea, the size categories are pekoe, orange pekoe, broken orange pekoe, broken orange pekoe fannings, and dust—the latter a low quality, inexpensive tea that finds its way into many of the world's teabags.

The graded teas are auctioned and exported, with the buyers relying on the expertise of their own tasters to guide them. The subtle variants of flavor in the vocabulary of tea are reminiscent of the argot wine-tasters use. Expert tasters classify tea into categories such as malty, pointy, bakey, thick, coppery, dull, and bright according to strength, flavor, and color.

The hill country where the best teas are grown is perhaps the most scenic part of Sri Lanka. Miles of lush green foliage and forest undulate across the hills and pickers move among the rows like vividly colored butterflies.

Dining in Sri Lanka

From street vendors to luxury hotels, eating in Sri Lanka is feast for all the senses

Douglas Bullis

Right:
Five-star dining in Sri Lanka is centered around the larger hotels and resorts on the south and southwest coasts.
Opposite:
A typical Sri Lankan breakfast might include (from left) milk rice, okra curry, string hoppers, plain and egg hoppers, steamed rice flour rolls, eggplant curry, and coconut gravy, with assorted sambols and fruits.

Breakfast in Sri Lanka is often a batter of rice flour cooked in special hemispherical pans to make *appa* or hoppers. These are small, bowl-shaped pancakes made by pouring a thin batter into the middle of the pan, then carefully rotating it so the batter climbs further and further up the side. The result is a soft, bready center and crisp brown edges that goes well with kitul-palm treacle and buffalo-milk yoghurt. Crack an egg into the middle of a hopper before turning the pan results in an egg hopper; these go best with thick, highly spiced *sambol*. Another rice-batter dish, called the "string hopper," is quite different. These are tangled little circles of steamed noodles usually served with a *hodhi* or thin curry sauce. String hoppers are jacks-of-all-trades, good any time of the day.

Sri Lankans lunch between noon and two, often with a plate of "short eats." These divide equally between crisply baked filo-dough biscuits and *frikadels* or deep-fried rolls or balls. The interiors are filled with meat, fish, or vegetables. Short eats are joined by *vadai*, or deep-fried donuts of lentils, spices, and flour. In the island's legion of "hotels" or fast-food restaurants, short eats come to the table as a tray filled with the house specials. The bill is determined by how many are left.

Another common snack is *roti*, a square or triangular wrap of dough stuffed with fresh chiles, onions, vegetables, and cooked egg, meat, or fish, which is fried on a searing sheet-metal griddle over a propane burner. Ask for a *kotthu roti* and the cook will chop up the *roti* as it cooks. The result is a meal that cools quickly—perfect for people on the go.

Many prefer a rice-and-curry lunch packet. Inside a banana leaf or thin plastic wrap is a cup or two of boiled rice, a piece of curried chicken, fish, or beef for non-vegetarians, or simply some curried vegetables. All this plus its *sambol* is priced so low they're the best value on the island.

Street vendors sit beside piles of orange-yellow king-coconuts. These are a variety that produces *thambli* juice, slightly sweet, aromatic, fruity, and

all using a single curry.

There are few native desserts but many *rasokavili* or sweets. *Kaum* is a battercake made of flour and treacle deep-fried in coconut oil. *Aluvas* are thin, flat, diamond-shaped halvas, or wedges of rice flour, treacle, and sugar cane. Coconut milk laboriously boiled down with jaggery and cashew nuts yields *kalu dodol*. *Kiribath*, a festive dish of rice cooked in milk, is the first solid food fed to babies. A dish that originated in Malaya is *wattalappam*, an egg pudding rather like flan. *kiri peni* or "curd and honey" is buffalo-milk yoghurt and treacle.

refreshing. (Green coconuts make a thicker meat layer but the juice is not so tasty.) The stall owner lops off its top with a scythe-like knife, then punches through into the interior with four quick chops until liquid spurts out. Sri Lankans simply tip it up and drink it with no glass or straw.

Evening meals at home are an exercise in the wife's formidable cooking talents. Each woman has her own spice blends for different dishes. Most women buy their spices in bulk and take just enough for a few meals to the grinding mills that dot every village and city. Rural women powder their own at home using stone mills called *kurakkan gala* (rotating mill) or *ulundu* (small mortar and pestle). A proper rice-and-curry dinner involves three or more accompaniments, at least two of them vegetables—women consider it lax to prepare them

Sri Lankans are not the restaurant-goers one finds in other countries. The dishes in most restaurants aren't that much different than those at home, so dining out is more for business occasions rather than family get-togethers. Restaurants are very popular for "Chinese" foods though. These were contributed to the cuisine by early Chinese who came to open small shopfront businesses, married locally, and taught their wives a few tricks. These days dishes like fried rice and chop suey are a tasty blend of both cultures. Thai and French cuisines are finding their way to the island to satisfy the palates of visiting businessmen. A fusion cuisine is even being created at some of the large international hotels.

Festive foods have religious overtones in Sri Lanka. From the moment Buddhism was introduced into the island in the fourth century BC, the monks were considered worthy of the best sustenance people could offer. In the ancient monuments, one comes across large stone "rice canoes" that the devout filled with rice and other foods as gifts to the monks.

In a similar spirit, today, the monks are hosted to *dana* or ritual meals served in private homes. These include the housewife's best dishes, some prepared solely for monks. On the first birthday of a child, the monks are served an elaborate meal in their begging bowls. When a monk has finished, he holds his hand over his bowl. The finale comes when the father of the child ties a white thread around the little finger of the senior monk, and then around the little fingers of every other person in the room, ending with the child, uniting the entire room in a spiritual bond.

Ayurveda is a philosophy of healthy living that has found its way into Sri Lankan cooking. The word comes from *ayur*, meaning "life" and *veda*, which means "wisdom." The Ayurvedic philosophy is that one's general well-being depends on one's choice of nourishment, lifestyle, and habits. Keeping these in balance is the best way to minimize health problems.

Ayurvedic theory states that overall health is determined by the combination of five basic elements that are consumed from nature: air, fire, water, earth, and ether. Everybody develops his or her own metabolic mix of elements by eating, drinking, breathing, and so on. Imbalances from the optimal state result in the various manifestations of poor health. Therapy involves prescribing a diet combining ingredients that restore the balance of these basic elements. Ayurveda turns up in the selection of spices for various foods. The average curry may contain up to thirteen key ingredients: onions, garlic, chiles, lime, turmeric, cumin, fennel, coriander, fenugreek, ginger, *rampe* (Pandanus), *karapincha* (curry leaf), and *sera* (lemongrass). Each of these has its own particular Ayurvedic effect as well as flavor.

Coursing through the cuisine of Sri Lanka is a great observance to details and tradition. It truly is like tasting history.

Herbs, spices, and other fruits are chosen by Ayurvedic health practicioners for the heaty and cooling properties in Ayurvedic medicine.

Part Two: Cooking in Sri Lanka

Sri Lankan kitchens retain a flavor of the past with the use of traditional utensils

Douglas Bullis

The traditional kitchen is at the back of, or separated from, the main house. Inside is a *lipa,* or open fireplace, with two or three trivets on which to place cooking pots. These trivets can be as simple as three stones, set tall enough to fuel a fire beneath, but just as often they are clay or metal tripods that do the same. Beneath the cooking area is a second shelf that holds the pots and fuel sticks to be used for that meal.

The fuel is usually the knotty stem of a fallen coconut frond. The leaves are stripped off and the stem is cut into lengths of about one meter or smaller. The fire is usually started with *kolapu,* the fibrous and highly flammable but long-burning mesh from which the coconut's flower originally blossomed—although a handful of dry coconut leaves will do in a pinch.

Once the fire is going, one or two stems are pushed into, or withdrawn from, the trivet beneath the cooking pot, making a simple but quite sensitive temperature control. A coconut frond fire has the added virtue of imparting a delicate scent of its own to the dish bubbling away in the pot.

Most rural homes have an oven of some kind, usually a cube of brick or iron, with a door in front and a fire pit beneath. Temperatures are hard to control, so the quality of breads and baked dishes can be rather uneven. Indeed, bread has never been a staple of the Sri Lankan diet, partly because of the rarity of wheat in this rice-dominated climate.

The traditional kitchen is quite a smoky affair, so it is usually ventilated with an open door or window and a clay vent pipe out the top. The fire area doubles as the storage place for oft-used cooking accessories like a pot of salt brine just above the fire area with a ladle in it. Maldive fish and chiles hang on cords to keep them dry. **Stoppered jars** hold dry seeds and nuts like jack and *cadju* (cashew). Since years of cooking smoke have turned the entire interior almost black, it is an ill-lit place even on the sunniest day, and requires kerosene lamps in times of rain and at night.

Nearby is the *mirisgala*—literally, "**chile stone**," though it is used for grinding many more items than chiles. The base is a heavy slab of granite or other very hard stone, about twelve inches wide, and half as long again, and at least a palm's width thick. Onto this the cook places chiles and whole spices such as coriander, cumin, fennel, turmeric and whatever else must be mashed to a pulp. Applying to these a stone roller as hard as the grinding-stone itself, the cook sits on a very low stool called a *hiramanaya*

Opposite:
An assortment of old pots and pans line the shelves of this period Dutch kitchen in the recently restored Historical Mansion in Galle on Sri Lanka's south coast.
Left:
The mirisgala, *or grinding stone, is still used today to grind spices in most kitchens.*

and shifts her body forward and backward from the waist, rotating the roller a little with each pass, until the condiments are perfectly pulped.

Other ingredients like cowpea or green gram (mung beans) may also need pulverizing but are too hard or large for the *mirisgala*. The cook then resorts to the *vangediya* or **mortar and pestle**. The mortar is a stone cylinder that reaches to her knees, whose mashing pit can be up to twelve inches in diameter and the same distance deep. The kitul-wood pestle can be up to five feet in length and is usually bound with an iron ring at the pounding end to keep it from slivering. Her rhythmic boom-boom-boom as she pounds with the pestle can be heard all over the village—a sure signal to a husband and children that dinner is on the way.

Glistening black **clay pots** are everywhere in the traditional kitchen, usually stored upside-down on a platform outside. The rule of thumb is, the older the clay pot, the better the flavors.

Some, like the *bath mutiya* or rice pot, have been shaped by centuries of experience guiding the potter's hand. It is a narrow-mouthed, chubby pot expressly made to heat rice until the water boils over. The erupting froth carries off chaff in the rice. The rotund shape ensures that the dripping froth doesn't fall on the fire.

A similarly refined pot named the *nambiliya* has the express job of separating the rice from the stones. The cook swirls the grains round and round in the pot and slowly

Above:
The hiramanaya, *or coconut scraper, is a short wooden bench with a metal extension and tooth grater.*
Below:
A wooden pestle and mortar is used instead of the grinding stone for ingredients liable to release juices.

ladles off the rice at the top, until only the stones remain.

The kitchen has literally dozens of other pots and associated implements such as **mesh** or **coconut-husk ladles**, shallow dustpan-shaped kulla **baskets** used to throw rice up into the wind to rid it of chaff, and the kalagediya or **water pot** which one sees everywhere being carried by village girls on their way back home from the well. Although unbreakable aluminum has superseded the more fragile clay, the *kalagediya*'s shape is the same: an almost spherical container the size of a basketball with a very tiny neck to keep the water from spilling on the way home.

Although no end of kitchens such as this can be glimpsed during a simple walk around a village, their charm is not matched by their practicality. The smoke, the soot, the heat, the inconvenient postures—all these have defeated any attempts at improvement.

One improvement, though, has stuck: the **propane stove** that one sees everywhere in the "fancy goods" or household-wares shops that line the streets of every village and city. Most are two-burner outfits, and quite economical compared with the enormous labor that accompanies traditional cooking methods. Propane stoves and kitchen counters are much better for the cook's health and posture, though they lack the built-in flavoring of the scent of a kitchen fire.

Cooking Methods

Despite a complex blend of spices, Sri Lankan dishes are simple to prepare

Douglas Bullis

Although Sri Lankan cuisine uses a complex blend of spices, and often requires several different cooking methods during the preparation of a single dish, it is much easier to prepare than some of the recipes would have you think.

Most spices take a different amount of time to release their flavor and aroma. Hence it is important to follow the correct order given when adding spices to the cooking pan. To be sure of maximum flavor and aroma, it is best to buy whole spices and grind them just before cooking. Heat the spices in a dry pan until they begin to smell fragrant, shaking frequently and taking care that they do not burn. Cool and then grind them in a small electric grinder or blender.

The spices are usually then sautéed or "tempered" in coconut oil, either alone or together with meat or vegetables. Most vegetable oil will substitute for coconut oil. Be sure to keep the temperature low and keep stirring the spices so they do not stick to the bottom of the pan. A wok is fine for sautéing. If a wok is not available, a large thick-bottomed skillet or frying pan will do.

After tempering, most vegetable dishes and curries are left to simmer over low heat. Close the lids only part way, since an important quality to a Sri Lankan dish is the rich sauce, which can only come about by letting the steam escape.

An exception to this is when using coconut milk, since coconut milk easily curdles or breaks down. It should be brought to a boil slowly, stirring frequently, lifting up a portion of the milk with a ladle and pouring it back into the pan. Once it has come to the boil, it should be simmered uncovered.

The seasonings can be adjusted just before the food is served. This may be as simple as a small sprinkle of the same spice used in the tempering, or the addition of fried mustard seeds, dried chiles, or curry leaves.

The centerpiece (literally) of the Lankan dinner is a fluffy bowl of rice, or *bath*. A rice cooker does almost as well the traditional *bath muttiya* pot.

Hoppers and pittu require specialized cooking pans. A very small wok can approximate a hopper pan, but it is best to try to find the real thing in Sri Lankan, or Indian, food stores. String hoppers can be approximated with an pasta maker using a vermicelli mold. Aluminum pittu steamers have largely replaced the traditional *pittu bambuwa*, as they are able to make five rolls of pittu at a time.

To make pittu *with a traditional* pittu bambuwa, *the flour and coconut mixture is stuffed into the bamboo which sits on a pot of boiling water. The steamed* pittu *are simply pushed out of the bamboo when cooked.*

Sri Lankan Ingredients

A guide to the products usually found in the Sri Lankan pantry

Belimbi

Cardamom

Cashews

BELIMBI (*billing*): Belimbi, a member of the starfruit family, is a sour fruit shaped like a tiny cucumber. Belimbi is a very common tartening agent which also has thickening properties. The fruit is sometimes soaked in salted fish brine before use.

CARDAMOM (*enesal*): Eight to ten tiny black seeds come from each straw-colored pod. Sri Lankans use only the seeds of the green cardamom, not the pods of the black cardamom. They must be freshly ground to give their true flavor.

CASHEWS (*cadju*): A rather garish fruit with a the familiar curved nut inside. Sri Lankan recipes that call for cashews require unsalted, unroasted nuts, as fresh as possible.

CHILES (*miris*): Green chiles are used in vegetable curries, and when finely sliced, in *sambols,* and tomato and onion salads. Red chiles are dried and either coarsely crushed for meat dishes, or powdered for fish and meat curries. Dried chiles are easier to work with if soaked for a few minutes in hot water. The small red, green, or yellow bird's-eye chiles (*kochchi*) are very hot. If the chiles called for

in a recipe are simply too hot for one's palate, either reduce the quantity or slice them in half lengthwise and discard the seeds.

CINNAMON (*kurundu*): The spice that launched a thousand ships is really dried tree bark. It is best not to use pre-ground cinnamon, which has little original flavor left; instead use whole sticks or grind them for the meal at hand.

CLOVES (*kambarunatti*): The "nails" of whole cloves are actually dried flower buds of an aromatic bush. The best are large and reddish-brown. Freshly powdered clove is a common ingredient in curries, while whole cloves are used while simmering curries, making savory rice, and in "devilled" or spicy-hot minced meats. Pre-ground clove loses much of the original flavor.

COCONUT (*pol*): *Pol* is the thick white meat scraped out of the coconut husk for dishes such as the spicy hot *pol sambol*. If packaged shredded coconut is too sweet, remove the sweet juices using a liquidizer.

COCONUT MILK: Coconut milk reduces the spicy tang of chiles. The recipes in this book call for two kinds of coconut milk. Thick coconut milk is made by grating the flesh of mature coconuts and squeezing it with about 1/2 cup (125 ml) water. For thin coconut milk, add about 2 cups (500 ml) water to the already squeezed mixture. Tinned and powdered coconut milk are widely avaiable in supermarkets and Asian foodstores.

CORIANDER (*kottamalli*): Small, aromatic coriander seeds are an essential ingredient in many meat and fish curries. Fresh coriander, or cilantro, is not as popular in Sri Lanka as elsewhere in South and Southeast Asia.

CUMIN (*suduru*): These tiny striped brown seeds can be used whole, but they are more often bought whole and ground just before use. The somewhat misnamed sweet cumin is not cumin at all but fennel (see below).

CURD: A kind of yogurt, made from the milk of the water buffalo, which has a considerably higher butterfat content than cow's milk. A popular dish in Sri Lanka is curd with treacle.

CURRY LEAF (*karapincha*): This delicately scented leaf is a very important part of a Sri Lankan cook's repertoire. The taste is a cross between basil and mint. It is almost always added when tempering (sautéing), as well as when simmering a curry under low heat. Usually an entire sprig of 8 to 12 leaves is used. It is sometimes available in dried form in Asian foodstores but the flavor is less pronounced.

FENNEL: Similar in appearance to cumin, fennel is often known as sweet cumin in Sri Lanka. Its fragrance and taste is similar yet milder than aniseed.

FENUGREEK (*uluhal*): The almost square, hard, yellow-brown seeds of this plant are used whole to make pickles and, after soaking, as a thickener in coconut milk sauces. Use sparingly as the seeds have a strong smell.

GAMBOGE (*goraka*): A thickening agent called for in many recipes, it also imparts a sharply sour taste. Tamarind paste is an acceptable substitute, but the dish must be thickened by another means such as using somewhat less coconut milk.

GARLIC (*sudu lunu*): In Sri Lankan cookery, garlic is minced or mashed before sautéing with other ingredients, to which are then added curries and the meat, fish, or vegetable ingredients. Asian garlics are somewhat smaller than Western, so a dish that calls for 3 cloves of garlic will do with two if cooked in Europe or North America.

GINGER (*enguru*): Sliced thinly, minced or crushed with garlic before tempering, fresh ginger is a flavor enhancer for meat and fish curries. The skin should be peeled before slicing or chopping it. Dried ginger is used more for sweets than for curries.

JAGGERY: The best jaggery is made from crystallized kitul palm sap. Palm sugar—

Cumin

Curd

Curry leaf

Fenugreek

Jaggery

Jackfruit (mature)

Lemongrass

made from palmyra palm sap—can be substituted. If none of these are available, use soft brown sugar even though the flavor will lack the complex nuances of the kitul sap.

JACKFRUIT: Jackfruit is a tough-hided fruit that can grow to enormous size. Generally, the bigger the jack the better the flavor. Recipes that call for young jack (*polos*) require that the fruit be scraped away from the tough skin and chopped or minced, seeds included. The fully ripe mature jack (*kos*) consists of two cooking elements, the pericarps or drupes, which are the sweet fleshy fruit, and the tender nut-flavored seeds. Both are used in recipes, but should be washed before further preparation.

KURAKKAN: Known as finger millet in English, *kurakkan* is a grain with a flavor and color similar to rye which is used in the preparation of some unleavened breads. Substitute with other types of flour.

LEMONGRASS (*sera*): Only the bottom 4 to 6 in (10 to 15 cm) of this rough-edged, stiff grass is used. It is sliced into lengths of about 4 in (10 cm) and cooked in fish and meat curries. It is a good idea to remove the weathered outer leaf and use only the tender core. Fresh lemongrass is becoming more widely available in specialty and Asian food-stores and is worth looking for. Powdered lemongrass does not have quite the same aromatic flavor.

LIME (*dehi*): There are several types of limes, but Sri Lankan recipes call for the thin-skinned, light green variety whose fruit is about the size of a walnut and is less acidic.

MACE (*wasawasi*): This carmine-colored latticework structure around the nutmeg seed is used in many curries, with or without nutmeg, whose flavor it resembles.

MALDIVE FISH (*umbala kada*): True Maldive fish is bonita dried in the roaring hot sun of the Maldives—it dries so hard it needs no salt. It is usually finely grated or powdered in Sri Lankan recipes. If Maldive fish is unavailable, freeze-dried fish flakes or dried shrimp can substitute.

MUSTARD SEEDS (*abba*): Sri Lankan cooks use both the tiny yellow and even tinier black varieties. Sometimes they are popped in hot oil before garlic and onions are added for tempering. Other times they are ground and added to a curry powder. They are also used whole in making pickles and cabbage dishes.

NUTMEG (*sadikka*): The nutmeg is a large tree with dense foliage that hides fruits the size of an orange. The ripe fruit splits in half, revealing the nut inside, covered with its drippy-looking husk of mace. Nutmeg is the material inside this nut. The whole nut is dried in the sun, broken open with a mallet, and the dried flesh is saved for grinding into curries or cookies.

Lime

OKRA: Also known as ladies fingers, okra acquires a slimy texture when cooked. This can be minimized by soaking them for five minutes in a bath made of the juice of one lemon in 4 cups (1 litre) of water. Pat dry and cook as normal.

PANDANUS LEAF: See screwpine.

PAPAYA (*pawpaw*): Although mainly consumed as a ripe fruit, wrapping meat in a papaya leaf or cooking a piece of green papaya with a dish greatly tenderizes the meat.

PEPPER (*gammiris*): Said to be the earliest-known spice, pepper is mentioned in Sri Lanka's ancient *Mahavamsa* chronicle. The pepper vine is a creeper that would otherwise be considered a parasite clinging to a tree. The corns grow in clusters that resemble tiny grapes. When ripe-red they are picked and dried in baskets in the sun (which can be seen on roadsides all over the island). Black pepper is the unprocessed dried seeds. White pepper is made by abrading the black skin off the corns in a coarsely woven basket.

SALT (*lunu*): Sri Lankan rural cooks do not use crystal salt, they keep a clay pot of brine directly above the cooking area, from which they ladle out as much as they want.

SCREWPINE (*rampe*): Pronounced "rampay," this blade-like shoot, also known as pandanus leaf, related to the shallot family is very often used as one of the ingredients tempered during the first step in making a curry sauce, and to add flavor to boiled rice. It is a tough and fibrous stem that can't be chewed, so must be remove before serving. Fresh and frozen screwpine leaves are becoming more widely available in specialty and Asian food-stores.

SWEET CUMIN: See fennel.

TAMARIND (*siyambala*): The dried seed pods of this large tree are rather sour, a taste that works well in some soups. The pulp inside should be soaked in water for a few minutes, then squeezed through a fine mesh to remove the fibrous parts and seeds. The pods are often chewed and sucked like hard candy by people working in the hot sun to keep their mouths from going dry. Tamarind paste is readily available in specialty and Asian foodstores.

TURMERIC (*kaha*): This small tuber is dried and powdered before doing double duty in recipes: first as pungent flavoring agent, and second as a color. If fresh turmeric root is not available, substitute 1/2 teaspoon turmeric powder for 1/2 in (1 cm) fresh turmeric.

VINEGAR: Rice vinegar is the best for Sri Lankan recipes. If it is unavailable, distilled white vinegar will do.

Mace

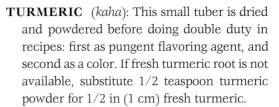

Maldive fish

Mustard seeds

Screwpine (pandanus) leaf

Part Three: The Recipes

Basic recipes for dips, pickles, curry powders, sauces, and stocks precede those for main dishes, which begin on page 42

Pol Sambol

Coconut Sambol (Mount Lavinia)

1 teaspoon finely chopped dried chile
1 tablespoon finely chopped onion
1 teaspoon pepper
1 teaspoon Maldive fish, ground (optional)
2 cups (500 g) freshly grated coconut
3 tablespoons lime juice
Salt to taste

Grind together the chile, onion, pepper, and Maldive fish. Add the grated coconut and season with lime juice. Mix well by hand to ensure all the coconut is coated. Best served freshly made.

Seeni Sambol

Onion and Maldive Fish Sambol (Mount Lavinia)

3 tablespoons oil
5 cups (1 kg) finely chopped onions
Salt to taste
8 cardamoms, crushed
2 in (5 cm) cinnamon stick
4 cloves
1 sprig curry leaves
2 in (5 cm) pandanus leaf (*rampe*)
$\frac{1}{3}$ cup (100 g) Maldive fish, ground
2 tablespoons chile powder
4 tablespoons tamarind juice
$1\frac{1}{2}$ oz (50 g) sugar

Time Estimates

Time estimates are for preparation only (excluding cooking) and are based on the assumption that a food processor or blender will be used.

🕐 *quick and very easy to prepare*

🕐🕐 *relatively easy; 15 to 30 minutes' preparation*

🕐🕐🕐 *takes more than 30 minutes to prepare*

Heat oil in skillet until hot and sauté onion, salt, cardamom, cinnamon, cloves, curry leaves and pandanus leaf until golden brown. Drain excess oil, leaving about 1 teaspoon in the pan. Stir in Maldive fish, chile, and tamarind juice, and sauté on high heat for 4 to 6 minutes until the mix is a dark brown color and the liquid evaporates. Stir in the sugar and immediately remove from the heat. Allow to cool before storing in sterilized storage jars.

Opposite:
Two or three sambols, or dips, are served with every Sri Lanka meal. Pictured here is an assortment of sambols from the Mount Lavinia Hotel.

Katta Sambol

Chile Sambol (Mount Lavinia)

2 cups (200 g) dried red chiles
Pinch salt
1 cup (200 g) finely chopped onion
3 tablespoons Maldive fish, ground
1 teaspoon lemon juice

Coarsely grind red chiles with the salt. Add all the other ingredients. Stir until well mixed. Store in covered container in a cool place and use as desired.

Kehelmuwa Sambol

Banana Blossom Sambol (Mount Lavinia)

2 cups (500 g) banana blossom
Lemon water made with juice of 1 lemon
    squeezed in 4 cups (1 liter) water
1 cup (250 ml) oil
1 cup (200 g) finely chopped red onion
3 green chiles, sliced finely
6 tablespoons lime juice
Salt and pepper to taste

Wash banana blossom in lemon water. Drain, pat dry, and deep-fry until golden brown. Mix together onions, chiles, lime juice, salt, and pepper. Add to the banana blossom and mix well. Store in covered container in a cool place and use as desired.

Kochchi Sambol

Bird's-eye Chile Sambol (Mount Lavinia)

$\frac{1}{2}$ cup (100 g) bird's-eye chiles
$\frac{1}{4}$ cup (50 g) finely chopped red onion
1 teaspoon pepper
3 tablespoons lime juice
Salt to taste

Combine chiles and onions and grind finely. Add pepper, lime juice, and salt. Best when served freshly made. Store in covered container in a cool place and use as desired.

Kalupol Sambol

Roasted Coconut Sambol (Mount Lavinia)

1 cup (200 g) grated coconut, roasted
3 red bird's-eye chiles, chopped
1 teaspoon Maldive fish
1 teaspoon pepper
2 cloves garlic, chopped
1 sprig curry leaves
3 tablespoons lime juice
Salt to taste

Blend all ingredients (add more lime juice if more liquid is needed). Store in covered container in a cool place and use as desired.

Dambala Sambol

Wing Bean Sambol (Kandalama)

$2\frac{1}{2}$ cups (500 g) finely sliced wing beans
Salted water for soaking wing beans
$\frac{3}{4}$ cup (150 g) grated coconut
3 tablespoons Maldive fish
$\frac{1}{2}$ cup (100 g) sliced onions
1 teaspoon crushed pepper
1 green chile, sliced
1 teaspoon lemon juice
Salt to taste

Soak wing beans in salted water for several minutes. Drain and squeeze out water. Mix all the ingredients together and adjust the seasoning. Store in a sealed container in a cool place until needed.

Karawila Sambol
Bitter Gourd Sambol (Kandalama)

8 oz (250 g) bitter gourd, sliced finely
1 teaspoon turmeric
³/₄ cup (150 g) finely sliced onion
2 green chiles, sliced finely
1 teaspoon Maldive fish (optional)
1 teaspoon lime juice
1 teaspoon salt

Rub bitter gourd slices with turmeric and fry them until golden brown and crisp. Mix the onion, chiles, Maldive fish, lime juice and salt together in a separate bowl. Add the fried gourd and mix well. Store in a sealed container in a cool place until needed.

Polos Pahie
Young Jackfruit Pickle (Kandalama)

1 lb (500 g) tender young jackfruit
Salt to taste
3 tablespoons vinegar
1 cup (200 g) chopped red onion
²/₃ cup (50 g) chopped green chiles
¹/₄ cup (50 g) sugar
2 tablespoons mustard seeds
3¹/₂ tablespoons chopped ginger
1 teaspoon peppercorns, ground
¹/₂ teaspoon garlic, chopped

Boil the jackfruit in a little water with salt and vinegar until it is just tender, then drain and retain water. Discard outer skin of jackfruit and slice thinly. Blanch the onion and green chile in the salt and vinegar solution. Mix onion and chile with the remaining ingredients, and add the jackfruit and some of the vinegar solution. Serve as an accompaniment to main dishes. Store in a sealed container in a cool place until needed.

Kathurumurunga Mallum
Shredded Agati Leaves (Lanka Oberoi)

A mallum is a dry mixture of shredded green leaves which is served as an accompaniment to rice. This recipe calls for agati (West Indian pea) leaves—*kathurumurunga* in Sinhalese—which is a common ingredient in East and Southeast Asian dishes, as well as in many herbal remedies. A mallum can be made with any green leaves such as manioc leaves, radish leaves, water convolvulus (*kangkong*), passionfruit leaves, and pumpkin leaves.

2 cups (500 g) finely shredded agati (West Indian pea) leaves (or other green leaves), washed well
¹/₂ cup (100 g) sliced red onions
1 tablespoon sliced green chile
¹/₂ teaspoon Maldive fish, powdered
1¹/₂ tablespoons lime juice
Salt and pepper to taste
1 sprig curry leaves
1 cup (200 g) freshly grated coconut

Place agati (or other green) leaves—together with any water that remains on the leaves after washing—and all other ingredients except coconut in a pan. Add a little more water if necessary. Stir well and cook over moderate heat, covered, for about 6 to 8 minutes. Add the coconut and cook, uncovered, several minutes more, stirring continuously. Remove the mix from heat and cool. Place in a sealed container and chill until needed. Mallums can be served hot or cold.

Unroasted Curry Powder (Royal Oceanic)

3$\frac{1}{2}$ oz (100 g) coriander seeds
$\frac{1}{2}$ teaspoon fennel seeds
$\frac{1}{2}$ teaspoon cumin seeds
$\frac{1}{2}$ teaspoon fenugreek seeds
$\frac{1}{2}$ teaspoon cashew nuts
2 in (5 cm) cinnamon stick
2 in (5 cm) lemongrass
6 cardamoms
6 cloves
$\frac{1}{2}$ teaspoon ginger
$\frac{3}{4}$ oz (20 g) peppercorns
$\frac{1}{2}$ teaspoon mustard seeds
3 oz (80 g) ground rice

Place all of the ingredients except for the ground rice in a blender and blend to a fine powder. Stir in the ground rice. Store in an air-tight container. If kept in a deep-freeze, this curry blend will remain fresh for a long period of time.

Roasted Curry Powder (Royal Oceanic)

$\frac{1}{2}$ teaspoon fennel seeds
$\frac{1}{2}$ teaspoon cumin seeds
$\frac{1}{2}$ teaspoon fenugreek seeds
$\frac{3}{4}$ oz (20 g) cinnamon sticks
6 cardamoms
3$\frac{1}{2}$ oz (100 g) coriander seeds
6 cloves

Dry-roast all the ingredients in a skillet until the mix becomes a deep golden color. Grind them to a fine powder in an electric blender. Store in an air-tight container. Sprinkle on vegetables and white curries prior to serving.

Kiri Hodi
Coconut Milk Gravy (Lighthouse)

1 tablespoon fenugreek seeds
2 cups (500 ml) chicken stock
1 Bombay or large red onion, finely chopped
2 sprigs curry leaves
2 pieces pandanus leaf (*rampe*)
3 cloves garlic, finely chopped
1 in (2$\frac{1}{2}$ cm) stick cinnamon
4 pods cardamom, crushed
2 green chiles, deseeded and finely sliced
1 teaspoon turmeric powder
2 teaspoons powdered Maldive fish
2 cups (500 ml) coconut milk
Salt and lemon juice to taste

Wash the fenugreek seeds and soak them in the chicken stock in a saucepan for 30 minutes. Add all the remaining ingredients except the coconut milk, salt, and lemon juice. Bring to a boil and simmer on very low heat until the onions are tender.

Add the coconut milk and heat the entire mix to boiling point, then reduce the heat and simmer for about 5 minutes. Remove from heat and cool slightly. Add lemon juice and salt to taste.

Saffron Lemongrass Sauce
(Yala Safari)

1 cup (250 ml) chicken stock
$\frac{1}{2}$ stalk lemongrass
1 thread saffron
1$\frac{1}{2}$ tablespoons lime juice
1 tablespoon cornstarch
Salt and pepper to taste

Boil the stock in a small pan with lemongrass and saffron, about 15 to 20 minutes. Dissolve the cornstarch in water, add to the stock and simmer 2 to 3 minutes until it thickens. Remove from heat, add the lemon juice, strain, and serve as an accompaniment to other dishes.

Melon Ginger Sauce *(Yala Safari)*

1 teaspoon fresh ginger, chopped
1 cup (250 ml) water
2 tablespoons cornstarch
7 oz (200 g) fresh melon, diced
1 teaspoon lemon juice
Salt and pepper to taste

Bring the ginger and water to a boil. Dissolve the cornstarch in small amount of water and add to the pan. Stir with a whisk while simmering for 5 minutes. Remove from heat. Add the diced melon and lemon juice. Season with salt and pepper and serve as an accompaniment to other dishes.

Chicken Stock

6 lb (3 kg) chicken bones, washed
6 quarts (6 liters) water
8 oz (250 g) onion, coarsely chopped
4 oz (125 g) celery, coarsely chopped
1 tablespoon coriander seeds, bruised
1 teaspoon black peppercorns

Place chicken bones into a large pot and just cover with water. Bring to a boil, then drain and discard the water. Cover the bones with the 6 quarts (6 liters) of water and add all the other ingredients. Bring to a boil, reduce heat, and simmer on low heat for 4 hours. Periodically skim the foam and oils from the surface. Remove from the heat, cool somewhat, and strain. This stock can be preserved in 1-quart (1-liter) containers in a freezer for up to 3 months.

APPA

Hoppers (Lanka Oberoi)

Hoppers—a favorite breakfast dish in Sri Lanka—are small bowl-shaped rice flour pancakes which are eaten with curries and sambols (it is usual to serve each person one hopper with an egg baked in its center and the rest plain). Although the traditional method of preparing them requires placing a hopper pan on hot coals (with more coals on its lid), hoppers may be prepared on regular stoves. Hopper pans are readily available from Indian and Sri Lankan foodstores. ✹✹✹

String Hoppers (below, see recipe page 114) and one Egg Hopper (above), accompanied by Coconut Milk Gravy (upper of two side dips, see recipe page 40) and Onion and Maldive Fish Dip (lower of two side dips, see recipe page 37).

3 cups (500 g) rice flour
¼ cup (60 ml) kitul palm toddy
    (⅓ oz or 10 g fresh yeast or 1 teaspoon dried yeast may be substituted)
2 teaspoons sugar
¾ cup (200 ml) thin coconut milk
Salt to taste
2 cups (500 ml) thick coconut milk

Combine the rice flour, toddy (or yeast), sugar, and thin coconut milk in a mixing bowl. Stir to form a thick batter. Cover with a damp tea towel and leave to stand overnight, or 6 to 8 hours, by which time the batter should have doubled in volume. When the batter has risen, soften it by working in the salt and thick coconut milk to form a thinner batter.

Heat a greased hopper pan (or any high-sided, small hemispherical pan with two handles) over low heat. Pour a large spoonful of batter into the pan and, being mindful to use oven gloves or pot holders, pick up the pan by both handles and swirl the pan so the batter rides up the sides almost to the rim. Replace the pan over the heat, cover with any saucepan lid, and cook until the surface of the hopper at the bottom is almost firm and the sides are crispy and brown, about 5 minutes.

Remove the hopper with a metal spatula (a curved instrument would be ideal) and serve hot. Grease pan again and repeat with remaining batter. Makes about 20 hoppers.

PITTU

Steamed Rice Flour Rolls (Kandalama)

Pittu are rolls of rice or ragi flour (*kurakkan*, a kind of millet) whose shape comes from having being steamed in tubes of bamboo. Pittu are classic breakfast items and are delicious when served with meat, fish, or vegetable curries. Sambols also make excellent accompaniments and they should be placed directly on top of the pittu so the grains will soak up the liquids. ◷◷

$^1\!/_2$ lb (250 g) rice flour or ragi flour (*kurakkan*)
$^1\!/_2$ lb (250 g) freshly grated coconut
$^3\!/_4$ teaspoon salt
$^1\!/_2$ cup (125 ml) water (only if needed)
$^1\!/_2$ cup (125 ml) thick coconut milk

Rub the flour, coconut, and salt together in a bowl to form small crumbs. Only add water if necessary (if using dessicated coconut, it will be essential to add some water).

Pack the crumbs firmly into a pittu or other cylindrical steamer about 3 in (8 cm) in diameter, and steam until cooked, about 5 to 10 minutes (the exact time depends on how firmly packed the rice flour is and on the size of the mold, so test and adjust times accordingly).

Unmold from the steamer and cut into 3-in (8-cm) pieces. Pour thick coconut milk over the pittu and serve hot.

PRAWN VADAI

Jaffna Prawn Patties (Lanka Oberoi)

Vadais are among the most popular snack foods in Sri Lanka. They are sold fresh and hot from street hawkers who patrol neighborhoods with their entire kitchen on the front of a bicycle, at cricket matches, in any fast-food restaurant—even on the trains by men who shuffle down the aisle hailing their wares in a staccato, "Wadi, wadi!" ⊘⊘⊘

1 lb (500 g) red (Mysore) dhal
$\frac{1}{3}$ oz (10 g) green chiles, chopped
$\frac{2}{3}$ oz (20 g) dried red chiles, chopped
$\frac{1}{2}$ lb (250 g) red onions, chopped
1 sprig curry leaves
$1\frac{1}{2}$ oz (50 g) Maldive fish, chopped
4 cups (1 liter) oil
Salt and pepper to taste
20 medium shrimp, peeled but with tails intact

Jaffna Prawn Patties (above) and Jaffna Pancakes (below; see recipe on page 115).

Wash the dhal and pick it over carefully to remove any stones. Soak for 3 hours, drain (reserve the water), and grind to a fine paste in a blender, adding a little of the water it was soaked in if necessary. Add the green and red chiles, onion, curry leaves, Maldive fish, salt, and pepper, and blend.

Shape into patties, 2 in (5 cm) in diameter and $\frac{1}{2}$ in (1 cm) thick, so patties resemble thick spectacle lenses. Each patty is called a vadai. Carefully press a prawn into the middle of each vadai until the prawn is firmly embedded. Heat the oil until hot and deep-fry the vadais to a golden brown. Remove with a slotted spoon, drain on kitchen towel and serve. Makes about 50 vadais.

HAL PITI ROTI & KURAKKAN ROTI

Onion-Chile Bread (Royal Oceanic) & Ragi Flour Bread (Yala Safari)

ONION-CHILE BREAD

It seems every roti maker has his own special way of turning and slapping a roti as it cooks. Rotis should be eaten hot; they quickly lose their quality as they cool. Leftover rotis can be crumbled and used as a soup enhancer, or as a thickener. This recipe makes about 10 rotis. ⊘⊘⊘

2 lb (800 g) roasted rice flour
14 oz (350 g) shredded coconut
1¼ cups (300 ml) water
1½ teaspoons salt
3 green chiles, chopped
2½ oz (75 g) onions, sliced
4 teaspoons small dried shrimp
10 curry leaves, finely shredded

Mix the flour and grated coconut together in a bowl. Add salt and enough water to make a stiff dough. Sauté the chiles, onions, shrimp, and curry leaves for several minutes until onions are translucent. Mix these into the dough and knead well.

Shape into 10 even-sized balls and flatten on grease-proof paper into circular shapes ¼ to ⅓ in (½ to 1 cm) thick and 3 to 4 in (8 to 10 cm) in diameter. Sear on a hot griddle or cast-iron skillet for 3 to 4 minutes then flip and cook the other side. Finish by placing both sides briefly above a naked flame. Serve with a meat or fish curry.

RAGI FLOUR BREAD

Ragi is one of the staple food grains in Sri Lanka, especially in the drier areas, and is higher in protein, fat, and minerals than rice or corn. It is often available from Indian and Sri Lankan foodstores. Makes 4 servings. ⊘⊘

10 oz (250 g) ragi flour (*kurakkan*)
10 oz (250 g) rice flour
1½ oz (50 g) shredded coconut
1 teaspoon salt
Water as needed
Ghee or vegetable oil as needed

Sift both varieties of flour into a bowl and mix with the coconut and salt. Add sufficient quantities of the water and ghee to form a stiff dough that does not stick to the hands. Knead well.

Shape into even-sized balls and flatten them into circular shapes ⅕ to ⅓ in (½ to 1 cm) thick and 3 to 4 in (8 to 10 cm) in diameter. Sear both sides on a hot griddle or cast-iron skillet, about 2 to 3 minutes each side. Finish by placing both sides briefly above a naked flame.

Clockwise from top left: ragi flour loaf (no recipe given), Ragi Flour Bread, Onion-Chile Bread, rice flour bread (no recipe given).

SWENDARA RICE & GAS GOLU BELLO

Aromatic Rice & Snails with Sorrel Leaves (Yala Safari)

AROMATIC RICE

Swendara, also known as cus-cus plant, is an aromatic grass (L. *andropogon muricatus*) whose roots impart a delicate aroma to dishes. The roots are also cultivated for their oil which is marketed around the world as the essential oil "vetiver." The best substitute is lemongrass. ☻

> 1 lb (500 g) *heeneti hal*, Basmati, or long-grain white rice
> 4 cups (1 liter) water
> $1/_3$ oz (10 g) *swendara* root, shredded

Aromatic Rice (left) and Snails with Sorrel Leaves (right).

Wash and drain the rice. Place in a pot with water. Add the *swendara* root (or lemongrass) and boil the rice until it is soft, about 20 minutes.

SNAILS WITH SORREL LEAVES ☻☻

> 1 lb (500 g) snails
> 1 cup (250 ml) rock salt brine (or heavily salted water)
> $1/_4$ cup (60 ml) white vinegar
> 3 teaspoons mustard oil or ground nut oil
> 1 cup (40 g) fresh sorrel leaves
> 1 cup (30 g) fresh mustard flowers (optional)

Wash the snails in several changes of water, then soak for 2 hours in salt brine (or salt water) and vinegar. Rinse them again in a large amount of water. Blanch them 5 minutes in boiling water and drain. Remove the snails from their shells. Cut away the alimentary tract at the end of the tail. Sauté the snails in the mustard oil for 3 to 5 minutes. Serve with fresh sorrel leaves, mustard flowers, and Aromatic Rice.

BATH RASAGULAWA

Delicious Cave of all Flavors (Mount Lavinia)

A specialty of Sri Lanka's legendary Chef Publis at Mount Lavinia Hotel, this dish puts onto one plate the best of the island's tastiest ingredients. It once was served only at the table of the Kandyan kings. ☺☺☺

3 tablespoons butter
$^3/_4$ cup (110 g) onions, sliced
5 cups (1 kg) *suduru samba* rice (any parboiled rice may substituted)
5 cups (1$^1/_4$ liters) Chicken Stock (see page 41)
2$^1/_2$ teaspoons salt
$^1/_2$ teaspoon ground pepper
Bouquet garni of 5 cloves, 5 cardamoms, 2 small cinnamon sticks, and 1 sprig curry leaves
4 cloves garlic, chopped fine
1 sprig curry leaves
5 cm (2 in) pandanus leaf (*rampe*)
$^1/_2$ teaspoon turmeric
3$^1/_2$ oz (100 g) lamb, diced or cubed
3$^1/_2$ oz (100 g) free-range chicken, diced or cubed
2$^1/_2$ oz (75 g) grouper or cod, diced or cubed
3$^1/_2$ oz (100 g) cuttlefish, diced or cubed
2$^1/_2$ oz (75 g) small shrimps
1 cup (110 g) diced carrot
$^1/_2$ cup (100 g) diced tomato
3$^1/_2$ oz (100 g) green capsicum (bell pepper), diced or cubed

Heat 1 tablespoon of the butter in a thick bottomed pan and add 1 tablespoon of the onions. Fry the onions until golden then add the washed rice, stock, salt, pepper, and the bouquet garni. Bring to a boil, reduce heat and simmer until the rice is tender, about 30 minutes. Remove the bouquet garni from the rice and set the rice aside.

Meanwhile, in a separate pan, heat remaining butter and fry the remaining onions, garlic, curry leaves, pandanus leaf, turmeric, and lamb until lamb is tender, about 25 minutes. Add the chicken and fry for 10 or more minutes. Add the salt, fish, and cuttlefish, and fry on low heat until the fish is tender, about 5 minutes. Add the shrimp, carrot, tomatoes, and capsicum. Mix well and simmer for 5 minutes more. Add the rice and mix well. Add salt and pepper to taste. Serve hot with side dishes of sambols and relishes.

KIRI BATH & GHEE BATH

Coconut Milk Rice & Ghee Rice (Mount Lavinia)

COCONUT MILK RICE

Hiding behind its simplicity of preparation, *kiri bath* is both a dietary staple and a food with ceremonial and spiritual significance which, according to historical evidence, has been a part of Sri Lankan culinary tradition for the last 2,500 years. Even today, it is the first food to be eaten on Sinhalese New Year when it is consumed with specially prescribed accompaniments, and it is also commonly eaten for breakfast on the first day of each month. ☺☺☺

Ghee Rice (far right) and Coconut Milk Rice (upper left), accompanied by Sour Claypot Fish (left dip; see recipe on page 68) and Chile Dip (right dip; see recipe on page 38).

5 cups (1 kg) glutinous rice
6 cups (1½ liters) thin coconut milk
1 cup (250 ml) thick coconut milk
½ teaspoon salt
2 teaspoons oil

Soak the rice in water for 30 minutes and drain. Place the rice in pan, add the thin coconut milk, and simmer on low heat for 30 minutes. Mix the salt and thick coconut milk and add to the boiling rice. Reduce the heat and cook until the rice is well done, about 10 minutes.

Smear a little oil on a banana leaf or a greaseproof paper, pour the rice on it, flatten the rice with a spatula to about ¾ in (2 cm) thick. Let cool, cut into diamond shapes and serve with Coconut Dip (see recipe, page 37).

GHEE RICE

3½ oz (100 g) ghee
1 medium onion, finely chopped
4 curry leaves
4 cardamoms, crushed
4 cloves
1 in (2½ cm) stick cinnamon
5 cups (1 kg) Basmati or other long-grained rice, washed and picked over
6 cups (1½ liters) Chicken Stock
1 teaspoon salt
⅓ oz (10 g) potatoes, cut into matchsticks, and fried
⅓ oz (10 g) roasted cashew nuts
1 teaspoon sultanas

Heat the ghee and sauté half the onion until golden. Add the curry leaves, spices, and cleaned rice. Fry over medium heat for 5 minutes, stirring continuously, then add stock, and salt. Bring to a boil, reduce heat, cover, and simmer for 30 minutes.

Meanwhile, in a separate skillet, fry the remaining onion and set aside to be used as garnish.

When the rice is cooked, remove the spices, place the rice on a platter and garnish with fried straw potatoes, fried cashews, sultanas, and reserved fried onions.

ISSAN SAMAGA WATTAKKA SOUP

Pumpkin Soup with Shrimp (Royal Oceanic)

A modern rendition of a basic vegetable and shrimp soup that goes well with any bread of your choice.
🕐 🕐

3½ oz (100 g) butter
3½ oz (100 g) onion, coarsely chopped
3½ oz (100 g) leeks, coarsely chopped
3½ oz (100 g) celery, coarsely chopped
1½ oz (50 g) garlic
¼ cup (30 g) flour
10 oz (250 g) pumpkin, cubed
4 teaspoons roasted coriander powder
4 teaspoons roasted cumin powder
3 teaspoons roasted chile powder
6 cups (1½ liters) Chicken Stock (see page 41)
Salt and pepper to taste
¾ oz (20 g) butter
½ teaspoon chopped garlic
15 medium shrimp, shelled
4 teaspoons sesame seeds, roasted
3 tablespoons roasted desiccated coconut

Pumpkin Soup with Shrimp (left) and Tomato and Fennel Soup (right; see recipe on page 116).

Melt the butter in a thick-bottomed pan. Add the onions, leeks, celery, and garlic, and cook slowly until the juices are released. Stir in the flour until the mixture thickens slightly. Cook several minutes to a blond-brown color. Add the pumpkin, then the coriander, cumin, and chile powders. Cover with a lid and simmer on low heat for 8 to 10 minutes. Remove the lid and add the warm chicken stock. Stir well and bring to a boil. Add the salt and pepper. Simmer 15 minutes and skim the soup. Remove from heat and blend smooth.

To prepare the shrimps, heat the butter in a pan and sauté the garlic. Add the shrimp and sauté briefly until shrimp change color, about 3 minutes. Distribute the shrimp and garlic evenly into soup bowls, add the pumpkin soup on top, and garnish with the roasted sesame seeds and desiccated coconut. Serve hot.

JAFFNA KOOL

Jaffna Seafood Soup (Lanka Oberoi)

Jaffna, in the north of Sri Lanka, is famous for its *kool*, or rich seafood soup. Originating from the Tamil fishing communities of the north, this soup is traditionally made with whatever leftover seafood is available, from crabs and shrimp to fish meat and fish heads. ☺☺☺

6 cups (1¹⁄₂ liters) fish or prawn stock, or water
¹⁄₄ cup (50 g) red (or other) rice
3¹⁄₂ oz (100 g) long beans, cut lengthwise
1¹⁄₂ oz (50 g) tapioca (or potato), cut into
    ¹⁄₂-in (1-cm) cubes
1¹⁄₂ oz (50 g) jackfruit seeds
3¹⁄₂ oz (100 g) jackfruit, cubed
1 teaspoon turmeric
¹⁄₂ teaspoon palmyra root flour (substitute with
    potato flour, or other strong flour)
Salt to taste
³⁄₄ oz (20 g) dried chiles, broken into pieces
¹⁄₂ tablespoon tamarind juice
1 fish head (about 1 lb or 500 g) of grouper,
    cod, or other mild-flavored fish
7 oz (200 g) flesh of the same fish, cubed
3¹⁄₂ oz (100 g) medium shrimp, peeled, with
    tails intact

In a large pan, bring the stock, rice, long beans, tapioca, jackfruit seeds, and jackfruit pieces to a boil, reduce heat and simmer for 5 minutes.

Add the turmeric, flour, salt, chiles, and tamarind juice, and simmer for a further 2 minutes. Add the fish and fish head, and simmer 10 minutes then add the shrimp and cook until shrimp are cooked, about 5 minutes. Serve hot.

BELI KOLA KANDA & POL KIRI KANDA

Bael Leaf Congee (Yala Safari) & Coconut Milk Congee (Lighthouse)

BAEL LEAF CONGEE

A *kola kanda* is an ayurvedic leaf congee which is eaten to prevent, or cure, a wide range of ailments depending on the leaves used. The mildly astringent semi-ripe bael fruit (L. *aegle marmelos*) is used to cure diarrhoea, while the leaves are said to to allay catarrh and fever. Since a *kola kanda* is often bitter, it is usually served with pieces of jaggery. *Kalanduru*, the rhizome of nut grass (L. *cyperus rotundus*), is a slightly bitter tuber which is also the base of many medicinal preparations. ☉☉

Clockwise from top: Curry Leaf Congee (see recipe on page 115), Coconut Milk Congee, and Bael Leaf Congee.

200 g (7 oz) long-grained rice
500 g (1 lb) freshly picked bael (*beli*) leaves
3¹/₂ cups (800 ml) water
1–2 slices nut grass tuber (*kalanduru*)
1³/₄ cup (400 ml) fresh milk
Pinch of salt
1 tablespoon kitul palm jaggery or palm sugar

Wash and drain the rice and then boil it in a generous amount of water until it is quite soft.

Wash and purée the bael leaves with the fresh water; pass through a fine strainer into the cooked rice. Add nut grass tuber, milk, and salt; mix well. Bring to a boil and simmer 3 minutes. Remove from heat and serve with kitul palm, or brown sugar.

COCONUT MILK CONGEE

Pol kiri kanda is often taken for breakfast, especially during the hot season as it is considered a cooling food. ☉☉

7 oz (200 g) long-grained rice
3 cups (750 ml) water
¹/₃ oz (10 g) ginger, sliced finely
³/₄ oz (20 g) onions, fried until crispy
3 cloves garlic, whole
Pinch of salt
1³/₄ cups (400 ml) thick coconut milk
1 tablespoon kitul palm jaggery or palm sugar

Wash and drain the rice, then boil it in a generous amount of water until the grains are quite soft.

Strain the rice and purée it with 1¹/₂ cups (375 ml) of the fresh water. Add the ginger, onions, garlic, salt, and coconut milk to the remaining water, and bring to a boil. Add the rice purée and simmer for 3 minutes. Remove from heat and serve with kitul palm sugar.

THORA MALU IŞTUWA

Seer Fish Lemon Stew (Lighthouse)

Seer, or Spanish mackerel, is arguably Sri Lanka's tastiest fish. Certainly it is one of the most popular with visitors, many of whom are accustomed to seeing it listed on the menu as pan-fried. There are, however, many other ways to bring out its delicious flavors, such as in this delicate stew recipe. ✪ ✪

1 lb (500 g) Spanish mackerel (*seer*) filets
   (substitute with kingfish or cod)
Salt and pepper to taste
1 teaspoon ground white pepper
5 tablespoons vegetable oil
3 Bombay or large red onions, 1 chopped and
   2 sliced into rings
2 in (6 cm) pandanus leaf (*rampe*), sliced
2 sprigs curry leaves
4 cloves garlic, finely chopped
2 green chiles, finely sliced
4 pods cardamom, crushed
$^1/_2$ teaspoon fenugreek seeds
1 in ($2^1/_2$ cm) lemongrass, finely sliced
2 teaspoons coriander powder
1 teaspoon cumin powder
$^1/_2$ teaspoon turmeric powder
1 cup (250 ml) coconut milk
Juice of 1 lemon

Season the fish filets with salt and pepper. Heat the oil until hot in a large sauté pan and sear the filets to firm the flesh, then set aside.

Reheat the oil and add the chopped onion (not the onion rings), pandanus leaf, curry leaves, garlic, green chiles, cardamom pods, fenugreek, and lemongrass. Sauté over medium heat until fragrant.

Add the coriander, cumin, and turmeric, and sauté until the oils are released and their aroma is strong. Add the coconut milk and bring to a boil. Lower the heat and add the onion rings and the fish filets. Simmer until the onion rings and fish filets are tender, about 15 minutes. Remove from heat. Cool slightly and add lemon juice to taste.

FISH BOLE CURRY & ADA MALU MIRISATA

Portuguese Fish Ball Curry & Kandian Eel Curry (Lanka Oberoi)

PORTUGUESE FISH BALL CURRY

A very tasty dish of spicy fish balls which are slowly simmered in an equally spicy curry gravy. ✪✪

1 lb (500 g) minced fish
1½ oz (50 g) red onion, minced
2–3 cloves garlic, minced
1½ oz (50 g) green chiles, minced
White from 1 egg
4 cups (1 liter) coconut milk
½ teaspoon Roasted Curry Powder (page 40)
2 teaspoons chile powder
1 teaspoon turmeric powder
1 sprig curry leaves
Juice of 1 lime
Salt and pepper

Kandian Eel Curry (left), and Portuguese Fish Ball Curry (right).

Place the minced fish in a bowl. Add ½ of the onions, garlic, and green chile, and mix well with the egg white. Make into balls about 1 in (2½ cm) in diameter.

In a large pan, combine the coconut milk, curry powder, chile powder, turmeric, curry leaves, and the remaining onions, garlic, and green chiles. Bring to a boil then reduce the heat. Add the fish balls, cover, and cook, stirring occasionally, until the fish balls are tender, about 10 minutes.

KANDIAN EEL CURRY

This classic fish curry from the picturesque town of Kandy is made from freshwater eels. ✪✪

1 lb (500 g) freshwater eels (*ada malu*), cut into 1-in (2½-cm) cubes
1 teaspoon chopped ginger
⅓ oz (10 g) green chiles, chopped
1 teaspoon fenugreek
2 teaspoons chile powder
2 teaspoons Roasted Curry Powder (page 40)
Salt and pepper to taste
1 tablespoon vegetable oil
1½ oz (50 g) red onion, sliced
2–3 cloves garlic, chopped
1 sprig curry leaves
2 cups (500 ml) water
Juice of 1 lime

In a mixing bowl, combine the eel, ginger, green chiles, fenugreek, chile powder, curry power, and salt and pepper, and mix well to coat the fish pieces. Set aside for 15 minutes.

Heat the oil in a large pan and sauté the onion, garlic, and curry leaves until golden. Stir in the fish mixture. Add the water, bring to a boil, then reduce heat to very low and simmer slowly until the fish is tender. Stir in the lime juice just before serving.

LULA FISH BEDUMA

Smoked River Fish (Yala Safari)

Lula are dark-colored freshwater fish that are often put into wells to rid the water of mosquitoes. This country-style dish calls for coloring lula fish filets with natural red and yellow pigments obtained from the bark of the *gammalu* and jackfruit trees respectively. The bark is soaked in water overnight, then each liquid is boiled in separate pans 2 to 3 hours. This coloring process may be omitted without affecting the flavor of the dish. ⓪⓪⓪

> 1 kg (2 lb) lula, cleaned and fileted (salmon, trout, or other firm-fleshed freshwater fish may be substituted)
> Sliced starfruit as garnish

Marinade

> 250 g (10 oz) starfruit, crushed
> 100 g ($3^1/_2$ oz) rock salt
> $^1/_2$ teaspoon honey
> 8 fresh sweet basil leaves
> $1^1/_2$ oz (50 g) garlic, crushed
> $^1/_2$ teaspoon turmeric powder
> 2 teaspoons chile powder
> 2 teaspoons lemon juice
> 4 cloves
> 4 cardamoms

Smoking ingredients

> 10 cinnamon sticks
> 4 cloves
> 2–3 drops cinnamon oil

Badum

> $^1/_4$ cup (60 ml) vegetable oil
> 1 sprig curry leaves
> 8 oz (250 g) red onions, sliced
> $^1/_3$ oz (10 g) pandanus leaves (*rampe*)
> 500 ml (2 cups) coconut milk

To prepare the **marinade**, mix all the marinade ingredients in a bowl and add the fish filets. Coat well, refrigerate for 8 to 10 hours. Remove fish, drain and pat dry with kitchen towel.

To **smoke** the fish, heat a wok over a low fire and add the cinnamon sticks, cloves, and cinnamon oil. Place the fish filets on a rack at least 2 in (5 cm) above the smoking ingredients. Cover and smoke for 10 to 15 minutes.

To prepare the **badum**, heat the oil in a pan and fry the curry leaves until aromatic, then add the onions and sauté until brown. Add the pandanus leaves and stir in the coconut milk. Place the smoked fish filets in the pan, cover, and simmer for 5 to 10 minutes at medium heat until the smoke aroma is absorbed into the gravy.

Remove from the heat, garnish with starfruit slices, and serve.

BALAYA AMBULTHIYAL & THITHTHAYA BEDUMA

Sour Claypot Fish & Deep-fried Battered Fish (Mount Lavinia)

SOUR CLAYPOT FISH

The southwestern coastal town of Ambalangoda first made this dish famous. A classic example of claypot cookery, the gamboge (*goraka*) or tamarind both imparts its characteristic sharp taste and also acts as a preservative. Even in Sri Lanka's heat and humidity, an ambulthiyal can keep for up to a week. Serve with plain rice. ✪✪✪

Sour Claypot Fish (left), and Deep-fried Battered Fish (right).

> 6–8 pieces gamboge (*goraka*), or 1 tablespoon
>   tamarind pulp soaked in 4 tablespoons
>   water
> 1 lb (500 g) tuna or other firm fish
> Juice of 1 lime
> 4 teaspoons chile powder
> 1 teaspoon ground pepper
> Salt to taste
> ½ cup (125 ml) water
> 6 cloves
> 1 slice of ginger
> 5 cloves of garlic
> 1 sprig curry leaves

If using gamboge, soak for 4 hours, or boil until tender. If using tamarind pulp, soak in 4 tablespoons water, stir and strain, discarding any solids.

Cut the fish into eight pieces, wash them well with the lime juice and arrange the pieces in a single layer in a pan.

Blend the gamboge (or tamarind water), chile powder, pepper, salt, and a little water to a paste. Mix this paste with the fish in the pan, coating each piece thoroughly. Add the cloves, ginger, garlic, curry leaves, and the water, and bring to a boil. Simmer until all the gravy has reduced and the fish pieces are quite dry, about 15 minutes.

DEEP-FRIED BATTERED FISH ✪

> 400 g (12 oz) *thiththaya* fish (small freshwater
>   fish, catfish or white fish may be substituted),
>   whole if small, or cut into small pieces
> Salt to taste
> Pinch ground pepper
> Juice of 2 limes
> 1 cup (250 ml) oil for deep frying
> 1½ oz (50 g) rice flour

Clean and wash the fish well. Cut into pieces of the size desired. Marinate the pieces with the salt, pepper and lime juice. Coat the fish in the flour and fry it in hot oil until tender but not too crisp.

SHRIMP IN COCONUT CURRY SAUCE
& STIR-FRIED SPICY SHRIMP (Kandalama)

SHRIMP IN COCONUT CURRY SAUCE
⊘⊘

2 tablespoons oil
3$\frac{1}{2}$ oz (100 g) chopped onion
6–7 cloves garlic, chopped
$\frac{1}{2}$ oz (15 g) chopped ginger
1 sprig curry leaves
2 in (5 cm) cinnamon stick
2–3 green chiles
2 teaspoons chile powder
1 teaspoon turmeric powder
4 teaspoons Unroasted Curry Powder (page 40)
1 large tomato, chopped
Salt to taste
1 lb (500 g) medium shrimp, peeled and
deveined, with tails intact
1$\frac{1}{2}$ cups (375 ml) thick coconut milk

Shrimp in Coconut Curry Sauce (left), and Stir-fried Spicy Shrimp (right), accompanied by Mango Chutney (circular dish, no recipe given) and Young Jackfruit Pickle (rectangular dish; see recipe on page 39).

Heat the oil in a pan. Sauté the onions, garlic, ginger, curry leaves, cinnamon, and green chiles until the onions are golden brown.

Add the chile, tumeric, and curry powders, the chopped tomato, and salt. Cook, stirring frequently, until the tomato is fully mashed, about 10 minutes.

Add the shrimp and simmer until cooked, about 3 minutes. Finally, add the thick coconut milk and bring to a boil again. Remove from heat and serve.

STIR-FRIED SPICY SHRIMP ⊘⊘

1 lb (500 g) medium shrimps, peeled and
deveined, with tails intact
Salt to taste
4 teaspoons coarsely pounded red chiles
1 teaspoon turmeric powder
1 teaspoon lime juice
1–2 teaspoons oil
7 oz (200 g) sliced Bombay onions
1 oz (30 g) sliced garlic
4 green chiles, sliced
1 in (2$\frac{1}{2}$ cm) cinnamon stick
1 teaspoon crushed peppercorns
1 small tomato, cut in wedges
1 sprig curry leaves

Marinate the prawns in the salt, red chiles, turmeric, and lime juice for 20 minutes. Heat the oil in a wok and quickly stir-fry the prawns at high heat until half done, about 2 minutes. Remove from the pan and set aside.

In the same pan, fry the onions, garlic, green chiles, cinnamon, pepper, tomato wedges, and curry leaves until crispy, about 3 minutes. Mix in the prawns and cook them while tossing to coat the prawns completely, for 3 minutes or until done.

GREEN SHRIMP CURRY & DALLO MALUWA

Green Shrimp Curry & Curried Cuttlefish (Mount Lavinia)

GREEN SHRIMP CURRY ✦✦

3¹/₂ oz (100 g) diced red onions
3 green chiles, diced
¹/₄ tablespoon turmeric powder
1 tablespoon Unroasted Curry Powder (page 40)
1 tablespoon chile powder
4 in (10 cm) pandanus leaf (*rampe*)
1 sprig curry leaves
2 in (5 cm) cinnamon stick
1 lb (500 g) freshwater shrimp, peeled
   and deveined, with tails intact
¹/₂ cup (125 ml) thin coconut milk
¹/₂ tablespoon mustard powder
¹/₂ cup (125 ml) thick coconut milk
¹/₂ teaspoon torn drumstick leaves
Juice of 1 lime
Salt to taste

In a large pan, mix the onions, chiles, turmeric, curry powder, chile powder, pandanus leaf, curry leaves, cinnamon, and shrimp. Add the thin coconut milk, and mustard powder, bring to a boil and simmer 5 to 8 minutes.

Add the thick coconut milk, return to a boil and simmer until the ingredients are tender, about 5 minutes. Add the drumstick leaves and remove from heat. Season with lime juice and salt to taste.

CURRIED CUTTLEFISH ✦✦✦

1 lb (500 g) cuttlefish, including heads
2 teaspoons oil
1¹/₂ oz (50 g) onions, chopped
1 sprig curry leaves
1 in (5 cm) stick of cinnamon
3 green chiles, chopped
1 teaspoon garlic, chopped
¹/₂ teaspoon chopped ginger
1¹/₂ teaspoons Unroasted Curry Powder (page 40)
Pinch turmeric powder
Pinch chile powder
1¹/₂ oz (50 g) tomatoes, chopped
Salt and pepper to taste
¹/₂ cup (125 ml) thin coconut milk
¹/₂ cup (125 ml) thick coconut milk

Clean and wash the cuttlefish, and remove the heads. Stuff the head into the body of the cuttlefish. Heat the oil and sauté the onions, curry leaves, cinnamon, and green chiles, about 5 minutes.

Add the garlic, ginger, curry powder, turmeric, and chile powder, and cook for a further 5 minutes.

Add the chopped tomatoes, and season with salt and pepper. Add the cuttlefish and the thin coconut milk, bring to a boil, and simmer. When the liquid is reduced by half, add the thick coconut milk, return to a boil, and cook until done, 5 minutes.

CRAB CURRY

(Lanka Oberoi)

Sri Lankan crab is famous throughout the region and rightly so. Fresh crabs, so plentiful in the seas here, are simmered to perfection in a spiced coconut curry gravy. Delicious! ☺☺☺

4 large crabs
3½ oz (100 g) red onion, sliced
2 green chiles, chopped
3½ tablespoons Roasted Curry Powder
   (page 40)
2 teaspoons turmeric powder
½ teaspoon chile powder
1 teaspoon fenugreek
2 pieces gamboge (*goraka*), chopped
1 sprig curry leaves
2 cups (500 ml) water
4 cups (1 liter) thick coconut milk
½ teaspoon mustard powder
Juice of 1 lime
Salt and pepper to taste

Clean the crabs, divide each into 4 portions, and place in a large pan. Add all the other ingredients except the coconut milk, mustard powder, lime juice, and salt.

Bring to a boil then add the coconut milk, return the mixture to simmering point, and simmer gently for 20 minutes. Add the lime juice, mustard powder, and salt, and stir for a few minutes until flavors are married. Remove from the heat and serve hot.

KUKULMAṢ KARIYA

Chicken Curry (Royal Oceanic)

Simple to prepare, this chicken curry tastes excellent with rice. ☯☯

3 lb (1½ kg) free-range chicken, cleaned and cut into 8 pieces
2 tablespoons oil
2 cups (500 ml) coconut milk
¼ cup (60 ml) warm water
1½ teaspoons salt

Marinade

1¾ oz (40 g) cashew nuts, roasted
½ teaspoon long grain rice, roasted
4 teaspoons desiccated coconut, roasted
4 teaspoons water
1 teaspoon chile powder, roasted
2 teaspoons fennel powder
2 teaspoons cumin powder
1½ oz (50 g) sliced onion rings
1½ oz (50 g) sliced tomatoes
½ teaspoon fenugreek seeds
2 green chiles, roughly chopped or left whole and scored
4 in (1½ cm) cinnamon stick
½ teaspoon chopped ginger

Chicken Curry (right) and Chicken Badum (left; see recipe on page 114).

To prepare the **marinade**, grind the cashew nuts, rice, coconut, and water in a blender until the mixture forms a fine paste. Mix this paste with the remaining marinade ingredients. Thoroughly coat the chicken pieces with this mix and leave to marinate for at least 20 minutes.

Heat the oil in a pan until hot. Add the coated chicken and sauté for 10 minutes. Add half of the coconut milk diluted with the warm water, and salt. Bring to a boil, cover, and simmer 10 minutes. Add the rest of the coconut milk and simmer, uncovered, until the mix becomes a thick gravy, about 15 minutes.

KALU KUKULU MALUWA

Black Fowl Curry (Mount Lavinia)

Once, this dish would only have graced the King of Kandy's table. Today it is a tasty, if less lofty, main course dish best served with vegetable curries, sambols, and condiments as accompaniments. ☺☺

2 tablespoons oil
1½ oz (40 g) onion, chopped
1 sprig curry leaves
2 in (5 cm) pandanus leaf (*rampe*)
1 in (2½ cm) cinnamon stick
3 cloves
3 cardamoms
1 teaspoon ground garlic
1 teaspoon ground ginger
1 teaspoon ground cumin
2 teaspoons ground coriander
½ teaspoon ground fennel
Pinch turmeric
2 lb (1 kg) black fowl, cut into 8 pieces
    (regular chicken may be substituted)
2 cups (500 ml) thin coconut milk
½ teaspoon tamarind juice
½ cup (125 ml) thick coconut milk
½ teaspoon mustard seeds
3–4 dill seeds
1½ teaspoons salt
½ teaspoon ground pepper
Fresh green and/or red chiles, sliced (optional)

Heat the oil until medium hot, add the onion, curry leaves, pandanus leaf, cinnamon, cloves, cardamoms, garlic, and ginger, and fry for 2 to 3 minutes. Stir in the ground cumin, coriander, fennel, and turmeric, and fry for a further 30 seconds then add the chicken and cook, turning the chicken pieces, until the meat is brown on all sides.

Add the thin coconut milk, bring to a boil, and simmer for 10 minutes. Mix the tamarind juice with the thick coconut milk, add to the curry, return the curry to a boil, and simmer for 12 minutes.

Meanwhile, in a separate pan, heat more oil and roast the mustard and dill seeds, then cool and grind to a powder in a blender. When the chicken is tender, add the ground mustard and dill mix, and the salt and pepper and stir well. Remove from heat and garnish with fresh chiles if desired. Serve as a main dish with rice and accompaniments.

SMOKED MEATS WITH WILD BERRIES, ROASTED YAMS AND FRUIT PUREE *(Yala Safari)*

This is a sophisticated form of *wanni* or bush dish whose roots may go back to the time of Sri Lanka's original Veddah inhabitants. It is best served without other accompaniments. ☺☺

> 1 lb (500 g) sweet potatoes, yams, or potatoes, cut into 1-in (2½-cm) cubes
> ⅓ oz (10 g) butter or margarine
> Assorted cold smoked (or roast) meats such as venison, beef, and ham, sliced
> Fresh berry fruits such as juniper, blackberry, raspberry, and strawberries as desired

Sauce
> ½ oz (15 g) chopped onions
> ½ teaspoon grated ginger
> 1 tablespoon butter
> Zest of 1 lemon and 1 orange, grated
> 2 teaspoons cornstarch
> ⅓ cup (100 ml) fresh orange juice
> 4 tablespoons fresh lemon juice
> 4 tablespoons port or red wine
> 1 teaspoon English mustard
> Pinch of salt

Preheat oven to 425°F (220°C, gas mark 7). Coat the sweet potatoes and yams with the melted butter and season with salt. Roast them in the oven for 1 hour. Remove and cool them for a few minutes.

In a separate pan, prepare the **sauce** by first sautéing the onions and ginger in butter until golden brown. Add the lemon and orange zest, and sauté for 1 minute. Add the cornstarch, using a wooden spoon to mix it well with the other ingredients. Cook this roux to a blond color. Add the orange and lemon juice, the port, and English mustard. Simmer for five minutes. Season with salt.

Pour the sauce into a sauce boat and serve with the sliced meats, roast yams, and strawberry or other fruits.

BEEF SMORE

(Lighthouse)

A dish of Dutch origin, beef smore appears in various guises throughout the region, wherever the Dutch maintained a presence during their colonial past. In Sri Lanka, beef smore is a real treat—a whole beef filet or loin which is slowly simmered in a spicy coconut milk gravy and then sliced and served in its own gravy. Eat with rice or breads of your choice. ✹✹✹

1 lb (500 g) whole beef filet or loin
2 tablespoons distilled vinegar
Salt and pepper to taste
2 tablesspons ghee or vegetable oil for sautéing
2 sprigs curry leaves
2 in (5 cm) pandanus leaf (*rampe*), sliced
1 in (2$\frac{1}{2}$ cm) lemongrass, finely sliced
1 shallot or Bombay onion, sliced
3 green chiles, deseeded and finely sliced
$\frac{1}{2}$ teaspoon chile powder
1 cup (250 ml) coconut milk

Pierce the beef all over with a fork or skewer and marinate in vinegar, salt and pepper for 2 to 4 hours.

Heat the ghee or oil very hot and sear the beef until lightly brown on all sides. This seals the meat and helps to retain the juices. Remove the meat from the pan and set aside.

To the same pan add the curry leaves, pandanus leaf, lemongrass, Bombay onions, and green chiles. Fry until half cooked, about 3 minutes. Add the chile powder and mix well. Return the beef to the pan and add the coconut milk. Stir well and simmer until the coconut milk reduces into a thick gravy and the meat is done to your liking, about 25–35 minutes.

Remove from the heat, slice the meat into the desired thickness, and pour the gravy over the slices.

MAS BOLA KARIYA

Creamy Curried Meatballs (Royal Oceanic)

Best served with rice and sambols. ☉☉☉

3 lb (1½ kg) minced beef
1 teaspoon salt
1 tablespoon chopped onion
¾ oz (20 g) green chiles, chopped
3 tablespoons oil for sautéing
7 oz (200 g) onions, chopped
3 tablespoons garlic, chopped
½ teaspoon ginger, chopped
12–15 curry leaves
¾ in (1½ cm) lemongrass
1 tablespoon chile powder
2 teaspoons ground fennel
2 teaspoons ground coriander
1 teaspoon turmeric powder
4 tablespoons tamarind pulp
2 cups (500 ml) coconut milk
3 teaspoons salt

Mix together the minced beef, salt, ½ teaspoon chopped onions, and green chiles. Using moistened hands, form the mixture into small balls.

Heat the oil to medium hot in pan and add the remaining onion, garlic, ginger, curry leaves, and lemongrass. Fry until brown.

Add all the powdered ingredients and fry for another 3 minutes. Add the tamarind pulp, coconut milk, and salt, and bring to a boil. Add the meat balls, lower the heat and simmer 10 minutes.

GONA MAS THELDALA

Tempered Venison (Mount Lavinia)

Venison, wild boar, hare, and game birds have always played an important role in Sri Lankan cuisine. In this recipe,venison is tempered with spices, sour belimbi and vinegar to produce a hot dry curry that goes equally well with plain rice or breads. ☻☻

2 tablespoons oil
2 tablespoons chopped red onions
4 in (10 cm) pandanus leaf (*rampe*)
1 sprig curry leaves
2 in (5 cm) cinnamon stick
1 lb (500 g) venison or other game meat, cut in 1^1/$_2$-in (4-cm) slices
^{1}/$_4$ tablespoon turmeric
Salt to taste
3 cloves garlic, chopped
1 teaspoon chopped ginger
2 tablespoons dried belimbi (*billing*)
2 tablespoons vinegar
1 tablespoon crushed black peppercorns
2^1/$_2$ oz (75 g) red onions, quartered
10 green chiles, halved lengthwise

Clockwise from top: Tempered Venison, papadams, Bird's-eye Chile Sambol (see recipe on page 38), and freshly grated coconut.

Heat the oil medium hot and add the chopped onion, pandanus leaf, curry leaves, and cinnamon. Fry until onions are golden brown.

Add the venison, turmeric, and salt, and cook over low heat, about 10 minutes. Add the garlic, ginger, and belimbi. Cook for a further 15 minutes depending on the size of the venison pieces (allow slightly longer for larger pieces). Add the vinegar, crushed pepper, quartered onions, and chiles. When the chiles and onions are half-cooked, remove from the heat, about 5 minutes.

ELUMAS & URUMAS CURRY

Spicy Lamb & Pork Curry (Kandalama)

SPICY LAMB ◷◷

2 tablespoons oil
3¹/₂ oz (100 g) onion, chopped
5 cloves garlic, chopped
1 oz (25 g) chopped ginger
2 green chiles, chopped
4 in (10 cm) lemongrass
1 in (2¹/₂ cm) cinnamon stick
2–3 cardamom pods, crushed
1 lb (500 g) lamb, cubed
6 teaspoons Roasted Curry Powder (page 40)
3 teaspoons chile powder
2 teaspoons turmeric powder
2 teaspoons ground pepper
2 large tomatoes, chopped
³/₄ cup (200 ml) thick coconut milk
Salt to taste

Spicy Lamb Curry (above) and Sour Pork Curry (below).

Sauté the onions, garlic, ginger, green chiles, lemongrass, cinnamon, and cardamoms in oil until the onions are golden brown.

Add the lamb and stir well to coat, then add the curry, chile, and tumeric powders, the pepper, and the tomatoes. Cook on medium heat until the meat becomes tender, about 40 minutes. Add the thick coconut milk, bring to a boil and simmer a few minutes longer, adjust the seasoning, and serve.

PORK CURRY ◷◷

2 tablespoons oil
3¹/₂ oz (100 g) onion, chopped
1 oz (25 g) garlic, chopped
1 oz (25 g) ginger, chopped
¹/₃ oz (10 g) lemongrass, chopped
1 lb (500 g) pork, cubed
3 pieces gamboge (*goraka*), ground (substitute with 2 teaspoons tamarind pulp soaked in 2 tablespoons water, stirred and strained)
1³/₄ cups (400 ml) water
2 sprigs curry leaves
4 teaspoons Roasted Curry Powder (page 40)
2 teaspoons crushed black pepper
2–3 cloves
1 in (2¹/₂ cm) cinnamon stick

Heat the oil in a pan and sauté the onions, garlic, ginger, and lemongrass until the onions are golden brown.

Add all the remaining ingredients, and bring to a boil. Reduce the heat and simmer in an uncovered pot until the gravy is thick and the pork tender, about 25 minutes.

THIBATTU BEDUMA & BRINJAL PAHIE

Tempered Eggplant & Eggplant Pickle (Mount Lavinia)

TEMPERED EGGPLANT

Thibattu (L. *solanum indicum*) are tiny round egg-plants (aubergines) which may not be readily available, substitute with pea eggplants. ⓧⓧ

500 g (1 lb) *thibattu*, substitute with pea
  eggplants (pea aubergines)
1 cup (250 ml) oil
5 oz (150 g) red onions, sliced
2 in (5 cm) pandanus leaf (*rampe*)
1 sprig curry leaves
1 in (2½ cm) cinnamon stick
½ teaspoon sliced green chiles
½ teaspoon ground Maldive fish
4 tablespoons coconut milk or water
½ teaspoon red chile flakes
Salt to taste
3 tablespoons lime juice

Tempered
Eggplant (below)
and Eggplant
Pickle (above).

Wash the *thibattu* eggplants then crush with a spoon. Fry in the hot oil until they lose their firmness.

In another pan, heat 2 tablespoons of oil, add the onion, pandanus leaf, curry leaves, cinnamon, and green chiles, and sauté several minutes until the onions are golden brown. Add the Maldive fish, coconut milk or water, chile flakes, and salt, and cook over medium heat for 5 minutes. Add the fried *thibbattu* eggplants and lime juice, and season to taste. Serve hot as an accompaniment to other dishes.

EGGPLANT PICKLE ⊘

2 tablespoons oil
500 g (1 lb) eggplant (aubergine), thinly sliced
1½ oz (40 g) onions, cut into rings
2 teaspoons mustard seeds, ground
1 teaspoon sugar
½ teaspoon turmeric powder
3 tablespoons vinegar
5–8 green chiles, halved lengthwise
2 tablespoons Maldive fish, ground
Salt and pepper to taste

Heat oil and fry eggplant slices until golden brown. Remove with a slotted spoon and set aside to cool.

In the same pan, add onions and sauté until soft. Add remaining ingredients and the fried eggplant slices. Cook for 10 to 15 minutes. Serve at room temperature. Serve as an accompaniment to other dishes.

BANDAKKA CURRY & ME KARAL

Okra Curry & Spicy Long Beans (Mount Lavinia)

OKRA CURRY ⏲

8 oz (250 g) okra (ladies' fingers), washed, tops
   removed, cut in 2-in (5-cm) diagonal slices
Pinch turmeric powder
1 cup (250 ml) oil
2 tablespoons chopped onions
1 sprig curry leaves
1 teaspoon Roasted Curry Powder (see page 40)
1 teaspoon ground Maldive fish
1 in (2½ cm) cinnamon stick
1 teaspoon dill seeds
Salt to taste
2 teaspoons lime juice
1½ cups (375 ml) coconut milk

Okra Curry (left) and Spicy Long Beans (right).

Rub the okra with turmeric (be careful as turmeric stains the fingers). Heat the oil and deep-fry the okra until light brown, set aside.

Place all of the other ingredients in a pan and bring to a boil. Reduce heat and simmer until onions are cooked, about 10 minutes.

Add the deep-fried okra, continue to simmer for about 5 minutes. Remove from heat and serve.

SPICY LONG BEANS ⏲

1 cup (250 ml) oil
1 lb (500 g) long beans, cut into 1½ -in (4-cm)
   lengths
3½ oz (100 g) red onions, finely chopped
2 in (5 cm) pandanus leaf (*rampe*)
1 sprig curry leaves
1 in (2½ cm) cinnamon stick
3 green chiles, finely chopped
Pinch of turmeric powder
2 teaspoons Roasted Curry Powder (see page 40)
½ teaspoon ground black pepper
½ cup (125 ml) thin coconut milk
½ cup (125 ml) thick coconut milk
3 tablespoons lime juice
Salt to taste

Heat oil and deep-fry long beans for 3 minutes, then set aside.

Reheat 2 tablespoons of the oil in a separate pan and sauté the onions, pandanus leaf, curry leaves, cinnamon, and green chiles, until onions are soft. Add the turmeric, curry powder, pepper, and thin coconut milk and simmer about 5 minutes. Add thick coconut milk and long beans, season with lime juice and salt, and simmer until remaining coconut milk evaporates.

POL BADA & KOS KARIYA

Heart of Coconut Palm Curry & Jackfruit Seed Curry (Mount Lavinia)

HEART OF COCONUT PALM CURRY

This dish is ubiquitous in Sri Lanka's "Coconut Belt" of *polgaha* plantations which grow the trees for their fiber, used in making coir rope. Periodically men called *pol kadana minihas* shinny up the trunks to lop down the nuts. As often as not, they bring down a budding spath for the plantation's cooks to turn into this dish. ☾ ☾

Heart of Coconut Palm Curry (above rice) and Jackfruit Seed Curry (below rice).

- 2 teaspoons ghee or oil
- 3½ oz (100 g) red onions, chopped
- 1 sprig of curry leaves
- 4 in (10 cm) pandanus leaf (*rampe*)
- 3 green chiles, chopped finely
- 2 teaspoons Roasted Curry Powder (see page 40)
- ½ teaspoon ground pepper
- 1 teaspoon turmeric powder
- 4 belimbi (*billing*), chopped
- 1 lb (500 g) white heart of coconut palm (*pol bada*)
- 1 cup (250 ml) thin coconut milk
- 1 teaspoon mustard seeds, ground
- ½ cup (125 ml) thick coconut milk
- 1½ teaspoons salt

Heat oil and fry the onions, curry leaves, pandanus leaf, and green chiles, until onions are golden brown. Stir in curry powder, pepper, turmeric, and billing, then add heart of coconut palm and thin coconut milk. Bring to a boil and simmer for 15 minutes.

In a separate small pan, mix the ground mustard with the thick coconut milk, then stir it into the curry and simmer 10 minutes more. Add salt to taste, remove from heat, and serve hot.

JACKFRUIT SEED CURRY ☾ ☾

- 15 jackfruit seeds, outer skin removed, cleaned and sliced
- 15 g (½ oz) minced onion
- 2 green chiles, sliced
- 1 teaspoon Roasted Curry Powder (see page 40)
- 3 tablespoons lime juice
- Pinch of turmeric powder
- 5 cm (2 in) pandanus leaf (*rampe*)
- 1 sprig curry leaves
- 1 cup (250 ml) thin coconut milk
- ¼ cup (60 ml) thick coconut milk
- 200 g (6 oz) tree spinach, roughly cut (regular spinach may be substituted)
- 1 teaspoon salt

In a pan, combine all the ingredients except the thick coconut milk, spinach, and salt. Bring to a boil, add the jackfruit seeds, return to a boil and simmer over a low heat until the jackfruit seeds are tender, about 10 to 15 minutes. Add the thick coconut milk and return to a boil. Add the spinach and salt, stir well, cook for a further 2 minutes, then remove from heat. Serve as an accompaniment to other dishes.

TANGY OKRA CURRY & PORTUGUESE OMELET

(Lanka Oberoi)

TANGY OKRA CURRY ◷◷

10 oz (250 g) okra (ladies' fingers), washed,
  tops removed, cut into 2-in (5-cm)
  diagonal slices
$\frac{1}{4}$ cup (60 ml) oil for frying
$3\frac{1}{2}$ oz (100 g) onions, chopped
1 teaspoon cumin seeds
1 sprig curry leaves
1 teaspoon turmeric powder
$\frac{1}{3}$ oz (10 g) green chiles, slit in half and
  deseeded
$\frac{1}{2}$ teaspoon fenugreek
2 tablespoons chile powder
$\frac{1}{4}$ cup (60 ml) tamarind juice
$\frac{1}{3}$ cup (100 ml) thick coconut milk
1 teaspoon salt

Tangy Okra Curry (left) and Portuguese Omelet (right).

Heat oil and deep-fry the okra until light brown, set aside.

Spoon 1 or 2 tablesoons of the oil into a pan and add all the remaining ingredients except the okra, tamarind juice, coconut milk, and salt. Sauté for 10 minutes on medium heat.

Add the tamarind extract and cook for a further 10 minutes over a low heat. Add the okra, coconut milk, and salt, bring to a boil and simmer for 10 minutes. Remove from heat and serve hot as an accompaniment to other dishes.

PORTUGUESE OMELET ◷◷

4 eggs
$1\frac{1}{2}$ oz (50 g) green chiles, chopped
$1\frac{1}{2}$ oz (50 g) red onions, chopped
$1\frac{1}{2}$ oz (50 g) tomatoes, chopped
1 tablespoon oil
3 tablespoons curry powder
3 tablespoons chile powder
1 sprig curry leaves
$\frac{1}{2}$ teaspoon turmeric powder
1 in ($2\frac{1}{2}$ cm) cinnamon stick
1 teaspoon fenugreek
1 tablespoon Maldive fish, powdered
4 cups (1 liter) thick coconut milk
1 teaspoon salt

Beat the eggs in a bowl. Add the green chiles, red onion, and tomatoes. Heat oil in a skillet and pour in the egg mixture to prepare an omelet. When set, remove from heat and cut into large pieces.

Place all the remaining ingredients into a pan and bring to a boil. Reduce heat, add the omelet pieces and simmer for 5 minutes. Season to taste before serving.

PARIPPU KARIYA & KIRIKOS MALUWA

Dhal Curry & Jack White Curry (Kandalama)

DHAL CURRY ☺☺☺

10 oz (250 g) chana dhal or yellow split peas
2 teaspoons oil
3½ oz (100 g) onion, sliced
½ teaspoon garlic, chopped
1 sprig curry leaves
2–3 dried chiles, roughly chopped
2 in (5 cm) pandanus leaf (*rampe*)
1 teaspoon mustard seeds, whole
1 teaspoon Unroasted Curry Powder (page 40)
1 teaspoon turmeric powder
⅓ oz (10 g) Maldive fish
½ teaspoon fenugreek seeds
4¾ cups (1200 ml) thin coconut milk
¾ cup (200 ml) thick coconut milk
1 teaspoon salt

Dhal Curry (above) and Jack White Curry (below).

Wash and soak the dhal in water for 30 minutes.

Heat oil in a pan and sauté onion, garlic, curry leaves, chile, and pandanus leaf, until onions are soft. Add the mustard seeds and fry for a few seconds until the seeds pop. Add dhal, powdered ingredients, Maldive fish, fenugreek, and thin coconut milk. Bring to a boil and simmer until dhal is tender, about 25 minutes. Add the thick coconut milk and salt. Simmer for a few more minutes while stirring. Remove from the heat and serve hot as an accompaniment to other dishes.

JACK WHITE CURRY ☺☺

1 lb (500 g) jack drupes (pericarps)
3½ oz (100 g) onions, chopped
½ oz (15 g) garlic, chopped
2–3 green chiles, chopped
1 teaspoon crushed pepper
½ teaspoon turmeric powder
2 teaspoons Unroasted Curry Powder (page 40)
½ teaspoon fenugreek
½ teaspoon Maldive fish
1 in (2½ cm) cinnamon stick
¾ cup (200 ml) thick coconut milk
1⅔ cup (400 ml) thin coconut milk
1½ teaspoons salt

Cut the jack drupes into large strips, remove the seeds and wash both the drupes and the seeds.

Place the onions, garlic, chiles, pepper, turmeric, curry powder, fenugreek, Maldive fish, cinnamon, and thin coconut milk into a pan. Cook on low heat until the seeds are tender, about 15 minutes. Add the drupes and thick coconut milk, bring to the boil, and simmer for 5 minutes. Remove from heat and serve hot as an accompaniment to other dishes.

AMBA MALUWA

Mango Curry (Kandalama)

A richly flavored, elegant classical Sinhalese dish that can be traced as far back as the fifth century, when it was served at the court of King Kasyapa of Sigiriya. ⊘⊘⊘

1 tablespoon oil
3½ oz (100 g) onion, chopped
1½ oz (40 g) garlic, chopped
½ oz (10 g) ginger, chopped
2 sprigs curry leaves
2 red chiles, sliced
4 teaspoons Roasted Curry Powder (page 40)
1 in (2½ cm) cinnamon stick
1 teaspoon salt
1 lb (500 g) green mangoes, peeled and cut into long, thick pieces
⅓ cup (100 ml) thin coconut milk
4 teaspoons mustard seeds
3 tablespoons vinegar
¾ cup (200 ml) thick coconut milk
1 tablespoon sugar

Mango Curry (above) and Pumpkin Curry (below; see recipe on page 116).

Heat the oil in a pan and sauté the onion, garlic, ginger, curry leaves, and red chiles until onion is soft.

Add the curry powder, cinnamon, salt, mango, and thin coconut milk. Bring to a boil and simmer until the mango is just tender, about 10 minutes.

Meanwhile, grind the mustard with a little vinegar to a paste. Stir the mustard paste into the thick coconut milk and, when the mango is tender, add the mustard and thick coconut milk, and the sugar, to the curry.

Bring to a boil, reduce the heat, and simmer for about 5 minutes. Adjust the seasoning. The gravy should be thick enough to thoroughly coat the mango.

KOHILA TEMPERADU

Tempered Yams (Kandalama)

Yams are among the ingredients that comprise *ambula*, the simple food of the country. Dishes like this are typically brought to the farmers working in the paddy fields by their wives or children. There, in the open air under the shade of a tree and accompanied by the sounds of the bell of the local Buddhist vihara, they mix their spicy yams with plain rice. This tradition gave rise to the dry cooking style with very little gravy so characteristic of country fare such as this. ☻☻

Tempered Yams (above) and Mixed Vegetables (no recipe given)

½ tablespoon oil
3½ oz (100 g) onions, chopped
1 oz (25 g) garlic, chopped
2 green chiles, chopped
2 sprigs curry leaves
1 teaspoon mustard seeds
1 lb (500 g) *kohila* yam (L. *lasia aculeata*), or
 other yams, washed and cut into fine strips
2 teaspoons fenugreek seeds
2 teaspoons chile powder
4 teaspoons Unroasted Curry Powder (page 40)
2 teaspoons turmeric
1 large tomato, chopped
2–3 pieces gamboge (*goraka*)
1 teaspoon salt
2 cups (500 ml) coconut milk

Heat the oil in a pan and sauté the onion, garlic, green chiles, and curry leaves until the onions are golden. Add the mustard seeds and fry for a few seconds until the seeds pop. Add the yam and all the other the ingredients except the coconut milk. Fry for a few minutes. Add coconut milk, bring to a boil, and simmer until the yams are tender, about 20 minutes. Remove from heat and serve hot as an accompaniment to other dishes.

BIBIKKAN

Mixed Spice Coconut Slices (Lanka Oberoi)

This dessert hails from the kitchens of the Portuguese colonial era. ☺☺

- **2 lb (1 kg) grated fresh coconut**
- **1½ cups (375 ml) coconut milk**
- **2 lb (1 kg) jaggery or dark brown sugar**
- **1 lb (500 g) caster sugar**
- **3½ oz (100 g) all-purpose (plain) flour**
- **7 oz (200 g) cashew nuts, chopped**
- **2 teaspoons mixed cloves, cardamom, and cinnamon powder**
- **½ teaspoon salt**
- **2 teaspoons grated lemon rind**

Bibikkan (right) and Sweet Coconut Jelly (see recipe on page 116).

Preheat oven to 325°F (160°C, gas mark 3). Dissolve the jaggery (or brown sugar) and caster sugar in the coconut milk. Place this liquid into a pan, add the salt and bring to a boil. Add the coconut pulp and cook until mixture is sticky but not burnt. Remove from the heat and slowly stir in the flour, mixing well. Stir in the cashews and mixed spices. Add the lemon rind and pour into a 9 in x 12 in (22½ cm x 30 cm) pan. Bake until done, about 30 minutes. The cake will be done when a toothpick pushed into the center has no batter sticking to it as it is withdrawn. Cool and cut into slices.

KONDA KAUM & BAMBI KAUM

Topknot Cakes & Coconut Cakes (Lanka Oberoi)

TOPKNOT CAKES

This deep-fried cake, sporting a topknot, is a popular snack or dessert. ⏱

- **1 lb (500 g) white rice flour**
- **2 cups (500 ml) treacle or dark brown sugar syrup**
- **4 cups (1 liter) oil for deep frying**

Topknot Cakes (no photograph of Coconut Cakes).

Using a fine sieve, sift the rice flour into a large mixing bowl and add the treacle. (If the mixture is too thick add a little hot water.) Set aside for 30 minutes.

Heat the oil to low temperature, about 300°F (150°C). Pour the mixture about ¼ cup (60 ml) at a time into the hot oil. After a few minutes the cakes will begin to stiffen. Insert a sharp-tipped wooden skewer or saté stick into the center of each cake and turn it in one direction while slowly lifting the batter out of the pan. The uncooked batter will emerge looking like a cookie with a topknot. When each cake reaches a dark brown color, remove from the oil and set aside to drain on absorbent paper to remove excess oil. Makes about 30 pieces.

COCONUT CAKES ⏱⏱

- **2 cups (500 ml) treacle or thick sugar syrup**
- **1 lb (500 g) grated coconut**
- **½ lb (250 g) green gram, roasted**
- **½ teaspoon salt**
- **3½ oz (100 g) rice flour**
- **3½ oz (100 g) roasted rice flour**
- **4 cups (1 liter) oil for deep frying**

Heat the treacle to simmering point and add the grated coconut. Stir continuously for 10 minutes then remove from heat and set aside.

Coarsely grind the green gram with a blender. Combine ground gram with the treacle and mix into a paste. Shape the paste into 1 in (2½ cm) round balls in the palms of the hands. Roll the balls on the rice flours until it coats them well. Heat the oil and deep-fry the balls until golden brown. Makes about 30 pieces.

CADJU TOFFEE & POL TOFFEE

Cashew Toffee & Coconut Toffee (Lighthouse)

CASHEW TOFFEE ⏲

2 lb (1 kg) cashew nuts
1 lb (500 g) sugar

Roast the cashew nuts in a slow 300°F (150°C, gas mark 2) oven until golden brown. Remove from the oven and cool. Crush the nuts into small, even chunks using a rolling pin.

Caramelize the sugar in a skillet. Stir in the nuts with a spatula. Oil a sheet pan, or stainless steel, or wooden table top and roll the hot nut mixture into a thin layer about ½ in (1 cm) thick. Cut into 1-in (2½-cm) squares and allow to cool.

Cashew Toffee (third row from left) and Coconut Toffee in three colors.

COCONUT TOFFEE ⏲

12 oz (350 g) sugar
1¾ lb (700 g) desiccated coconut
2 teaspoons cinnamon powder
¼ teaspoon clove powder
7 oz (200 g) cashew nuts, roasted and chopped
Pinch of salt

Place the sugar in a pan. Heat while stirring continuously until the sugar melts and begins to thicken. Add the coconut, cinnamon, and cloves. Stir the mixture until it pulls away from the sides of the pan. Add the cashew nuts and stir well. Remove from the heat.

Oil a sheet pan, or stainless steel or wooden table top, and roll the hot nut mixture into a thin layer about ¾ in (2 cm) thick. Cut into 1-in (2½-cm) squares and allow to cool.

BOLO D'AMOR

Portuguese Love Cake (Kandalama)

As the name implies, this dish is one of the culinary legacies of the Portuguese. Although it can be found throughout Sri Lanka, the origin of its name remains a mystery. ⊘⊘⊘

14 egg yolks
1 lb (500 g) soft brown sugar
12 oz (350 g) semolina, lightly roasted
5 oz (150 g) unsalted butter, softened
1 teaspoon rose essence or 1 tablespoon rose
  water
1 teaspoon vanilla extract or essence
¼ cup (60 ml) honey
1 teaspoon cardamom powder
10 oz (300 g) finely chopped cashew nuts
4 egg whites
Confectioner's (icing) sugar (optional)

Portuguese Love Cake (right) and Coconut Halva (left; see recipe on page 117).

Preheat oven to 300°F (150°C, gas mark 2). Grease a 8-in (20-cm) square baking tin or other cake mold and line with several layers of greaseproof paper.

Beat the egg yolks and brown sugar until creamy. Mix the semolina with the softened butter and add to the egg yolk and sugar mixture, and beat until well mixed. Add the rose essence, vanilla extract, honey, cardamom, and cashew nutes, and mix well.

Beat the egg whites until they form stiff peaks and fold into the mixture. Pour into the greased baking tin and bake for 1 to 1½ hours, until the top is browned and firm to touch. Remove from the oven and cool in the tin. Dust the top with confectioners sugar if desired.

Helpful hint: If the top of the cake is turning brown too quickly during baking, cover with aluminum foil. For a crusted cake, sprinkle a thin layer of confectioner's sugar over the cake before baking.

DRINKS

(Lanka Oberoi)

ORANGE AND CLOVE SHERBET ⏲

Juice of 3 oranges
1 lb (500 g) sugar
3 quarts (3 liters) water
2 cloves
2 cardamoms
Soaked tulsi (basil) seeds

Combine the sugar and water and bring to a boil with the cardamom and cloves. Simmer until reduced by half. Remove from heat, discard the cardamoms and cloves then add the orange juice. Allow to cool to room temperature. Float some soaked tulsi (basil) seeds on top of the drink as a garnish then chill before serving. Makes about 6 cups (1½ liters).

PINEAPPLE AND CINNAMON SHERBET ⏲

1 lb (500 g) pineapple
1 lb (500 g) sugar
3 quarts (3 liters) water
1 in (2½ cm) cinnamon stick
3 tablespoons fresh lime juice
Soaked tulsi seeds

Peel the pineapple, quarter it, and remove the fibrous core. Extract the juice from the pineapple flesh with a food mill or juicer. Set aside.

Combine the sugar and water and bring to a boil with the cinnamon stick. Simmer until reduced by half. Remove from heat, discard the cinnamon stick then add the pineapple juice. Allow to cool to room temperature. Float some soaked tulsi seed on top of the drink as a garnish then chill before serving. Makes about 6 cups (1½ liters).

(From the left) Iced Coffee (no recipe given), Orange Sherbet, and Pineapple Sherbet.

ADDITIONAL RECIPES

Kukulmas Baduma
Chicken Badum (Royal Oceanic)

This is a main course dish best served with vegetable curries, sambols, and condiments as accompaniments. See photograph on page 77. ⓓⓓⓓ

2 teaspoons chile powder
3 teaspoons fennel powder
2 teaspoons coriander powder
3 lb (1½ kg) free-range chicken, cut into 8 pieces
1½ teaspoons salt
2 tablespoons vinegar
2 tablespoons oil
1½ oz (50 g) onions, chopped
1½ oz (50 g) garlic, chopped
½ teaspoon ginger, chopped
1 sprig curry leaves
2 in (5 cm) lemongrass
¾ in (1½ cm) cinnamon stick
1 teaspoon mustard seeds
1 cup (250 ml) coconut milk

In a skillet, dry-roast the chile powder, fennel powder, and coriander powder for 2 minutes, until aromatic. Coat the chicken pieces with the spices, add the salt and vinegar, and set aside for 30 minutes.

Heat the oil in a separate pan. Add the chopped onions, garlic, ginger, curry leaves, lemongrass, cinnamon, and mustard seeds, and fry until the onions are soft and golden, and the mustard seeds pop. Add the chicken and gently sauté 20 minutes. Add the coconut milk, bring to a boil, and simmer until the chicken is tender, about 15 minutes. Toss occasionally so that the gravy covers the chicken with a thick, dry coating.

Idappan
String Hoppers (Mount Lavinia)

See photograph on page 43. ⓓⓓⓓ

3 cups (500 g) rice flour
1½ teaspoons salt
220 ml (1 cup less 2 tablespoons) boiling water, or as needed

Warm the flour in a low oven, then sieve into a bowl. Add the salt, then slowly add the hot water and work into a soft dough. Place the dough in a string hopper or vermicelli press, and press the plunger to squeeze small, flat noodle patties onto hopper mats.

Place the mats in a steamer, or a large pot with a trivet at the bottom and sufficient water to just reach the trivet's rungs. Steam until strings are fully cooked and springy in texture, about 10 minutes.

Remove string hoppers from the steamer and serve hot with Pol Sambol (see recipe, page 37) and Coconut Milk Gravy (see recipe, page 40).

Jaffna Dosai
Jaffna Pancakes (Lanka Oberoi)

This fermented bread originated in northern Sri Lanka but has now migrated to almost every corner of the country. Normally dosais are served with a few hot sambols on a stainless steel plate, or on a banana leaf. If desired, they can be stuffed with a richly spiced potato and dhal curry or a boneless chicken curry. See photograph on page 47. ⊘⊘

3½ oz (100 g) husked black gram
3½ oz (100 g) rice
3½ oz (100 g) wheat flour
Pinch baking soda (optional)
2 tablespoons oil
1½ oz (50 g) onions, chopped
2–3 dried red chiles, broken in two
1 sprig of curry leaves
½ teaspoon cumin seeds
½ teaspoon mustard seeds
1 teaspoon turmeric
1½ teaspoons salt

Mix the husked black gram (which will now be white) and the rice, and soak in a large amount of water for at least 2 hours. Drain and grind the soaked ingredients in a blender with enough water to form a batter of pancake consistency. Blend in the flour and baking soda (if desired), and leave to ferment in a large bowl for at least 3 hours (preferably overnight).

Heat oil and fry the onions, chiles, curry leaves, cumin seeds, and the mustard seeds. Add it to the fermented batter. Mix in the turmeric and salt, adding water if necessary to retain a pancake-batter consistency.

Heat a hot plate or griddle pan (or cast iron skillet) to high heat and smear a little oil on the surface. When the oil smokes, reduce the heat a fraction. Pour a ladleful of batter onto the hot plate, spreading it quickly, using a spiral motion, outwards until it measures about 6 in (15 cm) in diameter. Pour a few drops of oil on, and around the edges of, the dosai and cook it until lightly golden. Fold the dosai in half or roll it into a tube, and serve it hot with sambol accompaniments.

Karapincha Kola Kanda
Curry Leaf Congee (Lighthouse)

See photograph on page 61. ⊘⊘

7 oz (200 g) long-grained rice
1 lb (500 g) freshly picked curry leaves
3½ cups (800 ml) water
1¾ cups (400 ml) fresh milk
3 cloves
1 teaspoon salt
1 tablespoon jaggery or dark brown sugar

Wash and drain the rice, then boil it in a generous amount of water until the grains are quite soft. Wash and purée the curry leaves with the water, and pass through a fine strainer into the cooked rice. Add the milk, cloves, and salt, and mix well. Bring to a boil and simmer 3 minutes. Remove from heat and serve with palm or brown sugar.

Badapu Suduru Samaga Thakkali Soup

Tomato and Fennel Soup (Royal Oceanic)

See photograph on page 57. ☉☉

3$\frac{1}{2}$ oz (100 g) butter
3$\frac{1}{2}$ oz (100 g) onion, coarsely chopped
3$\frac{1}{2}$ oz (100 g) carrot, coarsely chopped
$\frac{1}{2}$ teaspoon garlic, coarsely chopped
$\frac{1}{2}$ teaspoon celery, coarsely chopped
1 oz (30 g) flour
10 oz (250 g) tomatoes, coarsely chopped
3 dessert spoons roasted fennel powder
6 cups (1$\frac{1}{2}$ liters) warm Chicken Stock
    (see page 41)
Salt and pepper to taste

Melt the butter in a thick-bottomed pan. Add onions, carrots, garlic, and celery, and brown lightly. Mix in the flour with a wooden spoon. Cook to a blond-brown color. Add the tomatoes and fennel powder, cover with a lid, and cook for 8 minutes on low heat.

Remove the lid and add warm stock. Stir well and bring to boil. Simmer 15 minutes and skim the soup. Pass through a fine strainer or liquefy. Return to pan and bring to boil. Season with salt and pepper to taste. Serve hot.

Wattakka Maluwa

Pumpkin Curry (Kandalama)

See photograph on page 101. ☉☉

1 lb (500 g) pumpkin, peeled, washed, and cut
    into medium chunks
3$\frac{1}{2}$ oz (100 g) onions, chopped
2–3 green chiles, chopped

$\frac{3}{4}$ oz (20 g) garlic, chopped
2 in (5 cm) pandanus leaf (*rampe*)
1 sprig curry leaves
1 teaspoon turmeric powder
$\frac{1}{2}$ teaspoon chile powder
2 teaspoons Roasted Curry Powder (page 40)
1$\frac{1}{2}$ teaspoons salt
2 cups (500 ml) thin coconut milk
2 tablespoons roasted and ground coconut and
    rice, mixed
1 cup (250 ml) thick coconut milk

Place all the ingredients except the ground coconut-rice mixture and the thick coconut milk into a pan, bring to a boil, reduce heat, and simmer until the pumpkin is almost tender, about 15 minutes.

Dissolve the ground coconut-rice mixture into the thick coconut milk. Add to the simmering curry and cook over low heat until the gravy is thick and coats the pieces, about 5 to 10 minutes.

Kalu Dodal

Sweet Coconut Jelly (Lanka Oberoi)

This jouncy jellied sweetmeat is a specialty of the region southward from the Buddhist pilgrimage town of Kalutara some 20 miles (30 km) south of Colombo. See photograph on page 105. ☉☉

12 cups (3 liters) thick coconut milk (from
    about 8 large coconuts)
$\frac{3}{4}$ cup (200 ml) kitul palm treacle or palm
    sugar syrup
1 lb (500 g) jaggery, finely grated (dark brown
    sugar may be substituted)
$\frac{1}{2}$ teaspoon salt
3$\frac{1}{2}$ oz (100 g) cashew nuts, broken into bits
1 lb (500 g) rice flour

Place the coconut milk in a bowl and add the treacle, jaggery, and salt, and mix well. Strain. Place the rice flour into a large pan and slowly pour in the coconut-jaggery mixture, mixing well. Add the cashews and bring the mixture to a boil, stirring continuously with a large metal (not wooden) spoon until the mixture is bubbling. Spoon off any oil that rises to the top of the pan. Cook the mixture until it gets dark and pulls away off the sides of the pan in a sticky lump.

Remove from the heat and flatten into a sheet pan and cover with greaseproof paper. Place in refrigerator to cool and stiffen. It should then become quite rubbery. When cold, cut into pieces of the desired size and serve.

Pol Aluwa
Coconut Halva (Kandalama)

Halva originates from the Middle East but traveled east to India and Sri Lanka where it became a very popular snack or dessert item. Although the town of Negombo thirty kilometers north of Colombo is said to be the original "home" of halva, or *aluwa*, in Sri Lanka, today this grainy fudge is found just about everywhere on the island. Aluwa are traditionally cut into narrow diamond shapes. See photograph on page 111. ⊘⊘

13 oz (400 g) rice flour
3½ oz (100 g) semolina
3½ oz (100 g) coconut, grated
7 oz (200 g) kitul treacle or dark brown sugar syrup
3 tablespoons water
3 tablespoons cashew nuts, chopped
3 oz (80 g) cashew nuts, halved
1 teaspoon roasted cumin seeds
½ teaspoon cardamom powder

Roast the rice flour, semolina, and grated coconut in a pan without burning. Boil the kitul treacle or brown sugar syrup with a little water, remove from heat and allow it to cool slightly. Mix the rice flour mixture into the kitul treacle. Add the cumin seeds, cardamom, and chopped cashew nuts. Pour the mixture onto a baking sheet lined with grease-proof paper, about ⅓ in (1 cm) in height. Dot the top with the cashew nut halves. Cut into narrow diamonds while still hot. Serve at room temperature.

ACKNOWLEDGMENTS

The recipes in this book were written by chefs at the following Sri Lankan hotels:

Kandalama Hotel
PO Box 11, Dambulla
T: 94-66-84100
F: 94-66-84109
E: kandalama@aitkenspence.lk
W: www.xasia.lk/kandalama

Chef Senaka Perera

The Lanka Oberoi
PO Box 252, 77 Steuart Place, Colombo 3
T: 94-1-437437
F: 94-1-447933
E: bc@oberoi.mega.lk
W: www.oberoi.mega.lk

*Executive Sous Chef
  KMR Morugama
Chef Leo Perera
Chef HB Piyasena
Chef KDML Niranjan
Chef Kishore Reddy*

Lighthouse Hotel
Dadella, Galle
T: 94-9-23744
F: 94-9-24021
E: jethot@sri.lanka.net

W: www.jetwing.net
*Executive Chef Mohan
  T Kulathunge*

Mount Lavinia Hotel
100 Hotel Road, Mount Lavinia
T: 94-1-715221
F: 94-1-730726
E: lavinia@sri.lanka.net
W: www.mountlaviniahotel.com

Chef Publis

Royal Oceanic Hotel
Ethukala, Negombo
T: 94-31-79377
F: 94-31-79999
E: jethot@sri.lanka.net
W: www.jetwing.net

*Executive Chef Gamini
  Thambugala*

Yala Safari Beach Hotel
PO Box 1, Tissamaharamaya
T/F: 94-47-20471
E: jethot@sri.lanka.net
W: www.jetwing.net

*Executive Chef Jayantha
  Ekanayake*

Special Thanks
The publisher would like to thank Mount Lavinia Hotel, The Lanka Oberoi, Jetwing Hotels Ltd, and Aitken Spence Hotel Management (Pvt) Ltd, for their generous support and assistance in producing this book.

Many individuals contributed recipes, information and assistance in preparing this book. We wish to thank Sanath Ukwatha, Bazeer Cassim and the staff of the Mount Lavinia Hotel; Ananda Yapa of the International Hotel School, Mount Lavinia for his endless patience explaining the fine points of Sri Lankan ingredients, and to Philomena de Lanerolle for typing them up; Stefan Pfeiffer, Narmada L Müller and Chef Helmut Hubele of the Lanka Oberoi in Colombo; Hiran Cooray, Kumara Seneratne and Ruvinika Seneratne of Jetwing Hotels, Ltd.; Gemunu Goonewardene and S Amal Nanayakkara of Aitken Spence Hotel Management (Pvt) Ltd; Mrs Indra Rani Lavan Iswaran for her assistance in the selection of recipes; Mario de Alwis of

Ma's Tropical Food Processing, Pvt Ltd; Ahsan Refai of Zam Gems and the staff of their shop at the Lanka Oberoi; Al-hajj MHA Gaffar and Al-hajj AG Kamal of the Historical Mansion in Galle; Lucky Perera of Lanka Hands for the use of backdop items in the photos, Ms Deloraine Brohier and Graham de Kretser for their information about the Dutch Burgher cooking traditions; Nissanka Goonasekera of Giragala Village in Mirissa; Mr & Mrs Shanti Perera of Sunray Beach Villa in Mount Lavinia; Mrs. Tissa Warnasooriya and PP Hettiarachchi of the Ceylon Tourist Board; George Michael of the Ministry of Tourism; and Lawrence Wheeler. Thanks also to Chefs Kishore Reddy and Jayantha Ekanayake for reading the manuscript and suggesting improvements.

Mail-order Sources of Ingredients

Most of the ingredients used in this book can be found in markets featuring the foods of Sri Lanka and India, as well as in other Asian foodstores and large supermarkets. Ingredients not found locally may be avilable from the mail-order markets listed below.

North America

A Cook's Wares
211 37th Street
Beaver Falls, PA 15010
Tel: 412-846-9490
www.cookswares.com

Curry Stuff
www.currystuff.com

Maha Bazaar
Tel: (301) 990 7425
www.mahabazaar.com

Penzey's Ltd
Tel: (800) 741 7787
Fax: (262) 679 7878
www.penzeys.com

SriLankaCurry.com
Tel: (888) 540 6090
Fax: (610) 239 0364
www.srilankacurry.com

The Spice House
Tel: (847) 328 3711
Fax: (847) 328 3631
www.thespicehouse.com

Europe

Bristol Sweet Mart
80 St Mark's Road
Bristol BS5 6JH
England
Tel: (0117) 951 2257
Fax: (0117) 952 5456
www.sweetmart.co.uk

Taj Stores
112–116 Brick Lane
Spitalfields
London E1 6RL
England
Tel: (0171) 377 0061
Fax: (0171) 377 6787
www.tajstores.co.uk

Australia

Manny's House of Spices
13 Ryedale Road
West Ryde, NSW
Australia
Tel: (02) 9808 1403
Fax: (02) 9807 7314
www.ammyspices.com

INDEX